Trying the Ties That Bind

Trying the Ties That Bind

ESSAYS ON SERVICE-LEARNING
AND MORAL LIFE OF FACULTY

David D. Cooper, editor

The Fetzer Institute · Michigan Campus Compact

ACKNOWLEDGMENTS

This project was made possible by generous support from The John E. Fetzer Institute, Inc., of Kalamazoo, Michigan.

The Fetzer Institute and the Michigan Campus Compact express their gratitude to staff who supported this project, especially Eleanor Greenslade, Lisa McGettigan Chambers, Jenni Bugni, Peggy Hashemipour, and Amy Smitter. Thanks also to Steve Berg, John Wallace, and Nelda Pearson who read early drafts of these essays and offered valuable suggestions.

Steve Esquith's essay "Coming to Terms with Political Violence through Service-Learning" is adapted from an article that first appeared in *Teaching Philosophy* (September 2000).

ISBN: 0-615-11883-6

Design and typography by Sharp Des!gns, Lansing, MI
Printed and bound by BRD Printing, Lansing, MI

C O N T E N T S

vii   Foreword

ix   Introduction

3   Coming to Terms with Political Violence through Service-Learning
Steve Esquith

23   Through *Grand Canyon* and Eastern Europe to *Habits of the Heart*: A Professor's Journey
Myron A. Levine

v

45 Stories and Reflections on Learning to Care
Margot Kennard

63 Professions of Faith
Roseanne Hoefel

105 Spirituality in the Service-Learning Design Studio
Virginia North

123 Community Service in Architecture and Urban Planning: Venues of Motivation
and Satisfaction
Kurt Brandle and Nancy M. Wells

137 The Roads Mistaken
David D. Cooper

✒

159 Contributors

F O R E W O R D

The nature and meaning of service in higher education has undergone a profound shift in a brief period of time. Michigan Campus Compact takes pride in the role it continues to play in making service an integral part of the life of college campuses. Most observers would point to the profound impact service-learning has on the lives and education of students. It is equally true that service in education can transform the work as well as the lives of the faculty. This transformation adds richness not only to individuals but also to the quality of education as a whole.

We at Michigan Campus Compact hope this publication engages faculty in exploring the bridges between spiritual formation, moral development, and active service. We owe a special thanks to the Fetzer Institute for making this publication possible, and also for their foresight to help deepen our understandings about the ways in which the inner life can be expressed in and through service.

We wish to give a special thanks to David Cooper, our editor and contributor, for his vision and commitment to this project. We challenge you to use *Trying the Ties That Bind: Essays on Service-Learning and Moral Life of Faculty* to explore and reflect on the ways in which service adds to your work and life.

AMY SMITTER
Michigan Campus Compact

I N T R O D U C T I O N

Lisa and Tony Chambers

The weekend before our wedding in 1996, we went on a retreat, partly to
escape the flurry of activity that built up before the wedding ceremony, and
partly to imagine and envision our lives together. The discussion about our
work lives lead to this project.

Lisa was the Director of Michigan Campus Compact, a collegiate
service-learning organization, and I was recently hired as a Program Officer
at the Fetzer Institute, a foundation involved in research and education
exploring the relationship between mind, body, and spirit. We wanted to
integrate our work lives and contribute something meaningful to our respec-
tive areas of work and our own individual and collective growth. The
thought of exploring the relationships between service, spirituality, and

moral commitment seemed right. It became quite clear that though our collective idea of a process to wed service and soul provided tangible enough scaffolding, we had little sense of what would eventually emerge from the process. We envisioned college faculty, staff, and students engaging in discussions about matters of spirituality, service-learning and their commitments to grow from that service.

We also imagined faculty writing about their personal experiences where service, soul, and their teaching vocation intersected. Admittedly, our enthusiasm was mixed with reservations about what we would ask of others that seemed so personal, intimate, even a little prying. Talking and writing about spiritual experiences and moral struggles, difficult within almost any context, seemed especially antithetical to the academic life. Lively prior conversations with trusted friends and colleagues, however, provided the right amount of courage—or naïveté?—to match our enthusiasm for the project. We stepped fully into the project as service and spirituality voyeurs and participants.

The Fetzer Institute and the Michigan Campus Compact provided the resources, staff energies, and encouragement to launch and learn from this wonderful opportunity. Those resources included grants to eight faculty in Michigan to explore and write about their experiences and struggles with the marriage of service, spirituality, and the teaching vocation. We met several times—including a three-day facilitated retreat at Seasons, Fetzer's retreat center—to share, critique, and refine the unfolding narratives and, more importantly, to give each other courage and continued freedom to write about matters of the spirit and heart. We are grateful to the Fetzer Institute and the Michigan Campus Compact for providing the means to get these stories out into the world where they will now take on a life of their own between the covers of such a visually inviting book.

Truthfully, our initial intention was not to publish a collection of essays, though we are delighted with this outcome, as well as the journeys that lead to the outcome. What we were primarily interested in was the response to an invitation to a specific group of people to form a learning community that creatively explored the marriage of service, soul, and vocation.

What has evolved from the project thus far is, at its humblest, an honest, if uneven, study of an emerging academic community based on the "strange freedom" of eight faculty from diverse institutions and disciplines to integrate service, spirituality, and vocation into their relationships and scholarship. While this monograph only partially fulfills the dynamics of this process, it succeeds as a collection of stories reflecting the struggles and deep wisdom inherent in the marriage of service, soul, and vocation.

Each essay, in its own unique way, responds to the question: "What story would college faculty tell if they could share where service and spirituality meet in their life's work?" The moral qualities that shaped the stories and inspired the community-building process among the writers seemed to be the same: tolerance, truthfulness, freedom, fairness, failure, respect, creativity, learning, love, connection, and belonging. Ultimately, the stories reflect what we often mumble as "wholeness" in the human condition. Wholeness in the true form that embraces both our individual and collective "light" and "shadow." Wholeness that accepts the simultaneous realities of togetherness and broken-ness. Wholeness that says that we are enough, in spite of, or maybe because of, our failures and successes, our shortcomings and long comings.

All of the writers contributing stories to the monograph share a common concern over *the struggle to make connections*: a struggle that cuts across themes of teaching, faith, vocation, and community-building. To varying degrees, each writer shows how service-learning pedagogy and philosophy help them to meet the challenges of bridge-building in their work as teachers, their duties as citizens, and as individuals seeking more satisfying and fulfilling inner lives.

Steve Esquith, for example, describes the struggle "to get [my] students to see the moral and political significance of violence from a more personal perspective"—a perspective, he shows, that is integral to "my own conception of myself as a teacher." His struggle for connection as a teacher is to instill in students—"jaded customers"—the courage and the insight to be effective and responsible public citizens. Like the other writers, Steve explores how service-learning is an ally in that struggle.

Myron Levine is similarly concerned with how his students can better serve the common welfare through heightened commitment to social and economic justice. Roseanne Hoefel struggles with ways to renew her vocation as a teacher through the models of faith provided by important elders in her life. Recognizing how important it is for students to "move beyond paternalistic service" when they engage in helping others in the community, Margot Kennard poses the tough question: "[W]hat does it mean to care[,] and how do we learn to care?" Virginia North, Kurt Brandle, and Nancy Wells search to improve connections between design students, their communities and built environments and, for Virginia especially, the parallel struggle to balance career, spiritual needs, and building community among her colleagues. David Cooper's story of struggle for connection is obvious from the subtitle he dropped from the final version of his essay: "Merging the Pathways of Profession, Community, and the Inner Life."

We appreciate and value the frustration David went through to find a title suitable for such an eclectic blend of essays. After many fits and starts, the title that finally emerged—*Trying the Ties That Bind*—manages to triangulate the main concerns of the monograph taken as a whole: the struggle for connection and completion, service-learning, and the search for personal wholeness.

We learned much from each other and the collective wisdom that grew out of our learning community. As it turns out, spirit is not about shouting from the highest mountain a thousand memorized prayers or meditations. It's about everyday acts of care, love, truth, and conscious service to others. It's about faith in the second-by-second, minute-by-minute, flow of life, and a deep trust that soulful acts will heal and transform life somewhere.

We also came to understand that "morality" is more a matter of human possibilities, hopes, and aspirations than the business of rules that prescribe some behaviors and prohibit others. If the stories told in this monograph do anything well, they show the moral life hard at work as each writer pursues what he or she esteems, cherishes, and finds endearing. In short, what puts their life *right*.

A final lesson: Service is not about an un-human or super-human act of giving, but about grace—the acceptance of being accepted—no matter what the act is. Service, according to Rachel Naomi Remen, that is a relationship between equals. A service whose intention is not to fix or incur in others a debt for the "help" they've received from me or us.

We are left with many more questions than answers—questions raised both within the written stories and among the story tellers. How is spirituality manifest in everyday acts of teaching and learning? Who determines what is spiritual? What moral fire resides inside individuals that draws them to particular serving relationships? For some, what keeps work and service "out there" away from matters of the heart? At what point do service and vocation blur and become the same thing? Is there ever a point at which serving and working are not spiritual?

We believe this modest book reflects a common struggle among people in any vocation and any relationship to quest for that which you really love, and, once attained, to wed yourself to it, making work, play, service, and self inseparable. Robert Frost describes that meeting place with characteristic clarity and simplicity in his poem "Two Tramps in Mud Time."

> My object in living is to unite
> My avocation and my vocation
> As my two eyes make one in sight.
> Only where love and need are one,
> And the work is play for mortal stakes,
> Is the deed ever really done
> For Heaven and the future's sakes.

Trying the Ties That Bind is good work. It's not perfect. Its essays do not queue up in a straight line. They are rhythmic, eddying, dissonant at times, but always with the right amount of tension. The monograph is eclectic in both text and character from essay to essay. It should not be viewed as a tamed piece of fine scholarship or listened to as a refined symphony, but rather as wild tapestry or a soul-stirring jazz improvisation. The writers are real and courageous teachers publicly working out their desires to say something meaningful about who they are and the work they love. It's what each of us struggles with every day.

Finally, this work invites your active engagement, not just with the stories of these writers, but with your own story. The wish that we have for each of you who choose to read the following pages is that you find the story you want to tell in the sharing of these eight journeys.

R̃c

Trying the Ties That Bind

Coming to Terms with Political Violence
through Service-Learning

Steve Esquith

Education is what happens to the other person, not what comes out of the mouth of the educator. —*Myles Horton*

In 1959 J. Glenn Gray wrote *The Warriors: Reflections on Men in Battle*, a memoir of his experience as an Allied interrogation officer in World War II. Throughout the book Gray emphasizes the similarities between the sometimes erotic, sometimes callous feelings of soldiers and citizens in general toward violence. It is a frank and disturbing indictment of a culture of violence that was reissued in 1970 during the Vietnam War when Gray was reminded of how virulent an abstract hatred of the enemy can become the farther away you are from actual combat. To my mind the most unsettling idea in the book is Gray's thesis about the relationship between violence and politics. One reason we have so much difficulty coming to terms with violence in modern Western societies, he argues, is that those who are supposed to control violence often cover it up. According to Gray, "sometimes it takes penetrating eyes to notice the violent undercurrents of daily life in our Western society, so commonplace do they seem and so adept are public officials in keeping the more overt out of sight." In wartime, political leaders may deny that they have done intentional harm to civilian populations, our own as well as the enemy's. In peacetime, they may deny police brutality. Short of sheer denial, statistics can be manipulated, silence can be bought, and those who suffer from violence can be cleverly disenfranchised or buried in committee. The cumulative effect is what Gray calls an "atmosphere of violence" that "draws a veil over our eyes, preventing us from seeing the plainest facts of our daily existence." Not all violence is political in this sense, but in modern Western societies it often is.

Now, at the turn of the century, it no longer requires "penetrating eyes" to see political violence. The "veil" has been lifted, and no one, certainly not "public officials," tries to keep violence—from domestic abuse to terrorist bombings to grinding ethnic cleansing—"out of sight." Instead, political leaders and bureaucrats speak casually of the need to cope with the effects of violence and manage the risk of violence within acceptable limits. Stathis Gourgouris comments on this phenomenon in "Enlightenment and *Paranomia,*" an essay in Hent de Vries and Samuel Weber's *Violence, Identity, and Self-Determination.* "Not long ago the President of the United States, in a tone that suggested presiding over the closing ceremonies of the twentieth century," Gourgouris writes, "publicly admitted that the country he was chosen to lead is the world's most violent society. He offered this insight as he would announce another self-evident fact, such as the country's ever accumulating debt or its inviolable entrepreneurial spirit." Violence is now a routine part of the cost of doing political business. It is just "collateral damage," and this makes the problem of political violence today even more urgent than Gray thought it was.

The Warriors is often used in university courses on war and morality because it provides students with a vocabulary for discussing the concrete details of war. Most of my students in 1998, however, found it "boring." If we are going to make violence less "boring" to our students without being merely entertaining, we will have to teach them to recognize that it is not just another form of deficit spending. This essay is about their political education as jaded consumers and one attempt I've made to get them to see the moral and political significance of violence from a more personal perspective.

This emphasis on political education is central to my own conception of myself as a teacher. Although as a university professor, I do political philosophy when I write books and articles and attend academic conferences, I do not think of myself as a political philosopher the same way that most of my colleagues think of themselves as logicians or moral philosophers. They take great pleasure in solving logical problems or uncovering metaphysical commitments. What keeps me going is the belief, however pious, that democratic political philosophy is a needed form of political education in modern societies where consumerism and professional authority have blinded us to political violence. Because some political philosophers have exacerbated the problem of political violence while most have ignored it, those of us in the trade who value democratic citizenship have a duty to see what can be done to mitigate it.

Most of my students have been undergraduate and graduate students at Michigan State University, but I have also taught prison inmates, illiterate adults, advanced high school students, labor union shop stewards, and even elementary school students. Of course, the readings and approaches that I have used have varied considerably. With the exception of the last group, the goal has been the same. I have tried to show students that they already speak the language of democracy, that they know how to participate in public life, and that the obstacles to more informed participation are significant but not insurmountable. I also have tried, with less success, to help them better understand the place of violence in democratic politics so that they do not think that a romantic or pastoral ideal of democracy is the only alternative to consumerism and dependence upon professional authority. The service-learning project in the course that I teach on war and morality is designed specifically for this last purpose.

Coming to terms with political violence is not usually thought of as form of public spiritedness. When we—democratic citizens in the United States in the twenty-first century—think of public spiritedness, we usually think of a willingness to sacrifice economic interest or partisan political advantage for the sake of some public good or even a more elusive notion of the common good. The argument of this essay is that public spirit in a democratic society should involve more than compassion, empathy, and a willingness to fight the good fight when the time comes. Democratic public spirit also involves a feel for the violent currents that run through the legitimate exercise of state power and the ability to handle this burden in a cooperative way. Democratic public spirit requires a kind of poise or composure under fire that neither liberal nor communitarian theories of democratic politics have captured.

To call democratic public spirit a martial virtue would be misleading, but it is certainly sometimes evident in war. In his story "The Things They Carried," Tim O'Brien reflects on the weight of the burden he and the other members of his Vietnam combat platoon had to carry everyday.

For the most part they carried themselves with poise, a kind of dignity.
Now and then, however, there were times of panic, when they squealed
or wanted to squeal but couldn't, when they twitched and made moan-
ing sounds and covered their heads and said Dear Jesus and flopped
around on the earth and fired their weapons blindly and cringed and
sobbed and begged for the noise to stop and went wild and made stupid
promises to themselves and to God and to their mothers and fathers,
hoping not to die. In different ways, it happened to all of them. After-
ward, when the firing ended, they would blink and peek up. They would
touch their bodies, feeling shame, then quickly hiding it. They would
force themselves to stand. As if in slow motion, frame by frame, the
world would take on the old logic—absolute silence, then the wind, then
sunlight, then voices. It was the burden of being alive. Awkwardly, the
men would reassemble themselves, first in private, then in groups,
becoming soldiers again.

The public spirit of democratic citizens is not bravado. It is the capacity to pull yourself together for another march, another meeting, another
acrimonious debate, or even another betrayal. It is being able to name the
denials and obfuscations of public officials and then sit down with them to
fix things. It is being able to stick with it for what Myles Horton called the
long haul: "If you believe in democracy," Horton writes in his autobiography, "which I do, you have to believe that people have the capacity within
themselves to develop the ability to govern themselves. You've got to believe
in that potential, and to work as if it were true in the situation."

Weaving public service into my own teaching has helped me avoid
denying the painful existence of political violence in democracy and given
me a way to convey this aspect of public spiritedness to my students. If

there can be only one spiritual element in democratic citizenship, let it be this stoic attitude toward political violence. If there is a patron saint for this kind of democratic spirituality, it may be Ralph Waldo Emerson whose skepticism toward government authority was matched by a deep commitment to democratic citizenship. The Fugitive Slave Law represented in Emerson's day a clear case of political violence. His response to it was unequivocal. "[N]o forms, neither constitutions, nor laws, nor covenants, nor churches, nor bibles," Emerson claims in "The Fugitive Slave Law," "are of any use in themselves. The Devil nestles comfortably into them all. There is no help but in the head and heart and hamstrings of a man. Covenants are of no use without honest men to keep them; laws of none but with loyal citizens to obey them."

In the first section of this essay I review those events in my own life that led me to the belief that political philosophy should help citizens come to terms with political violence. Next, I discuss the notion of the political responsibility of the political philosopher more generally, comparing the way in which service-learning in applied ethics courses may meet the social responsibilities of the moral philosopher with the way that service-learning in a political philosophy course may function to meet the responsibilities of the political philosopher. I then return to my own efforts to teach political philosophy as a form of political education, reviewing the particular service-learning option that I used in my general education course on war and morality.

POLITICAL EDUCATION

My first encounter with the demands of democratic citizenship occurred as an undergraduate during the Vietnam War. After registering for the draft, I wrote a long letter explaining my opposition to the war to my uncle, a combat veteran of World War II whose mother had lost her parents and siblings in Nazi concentration camps. While he and I never saw eye to eye, the letters we exchanged helped me understand the limits of my own emerging beliefs more clearly. On the basis of these beliefs, I joined a local non-violent protest group, and I sat in at draft boards and military installations. Around this time I also worked as a volunteer for the Elizabeth Peabody Settlement House in Somerville, Massachusetts, counseling high school drop-outs.

I didn't have a clear view about the connection between these two activities, even though the Somerville kids I got to know were unabashedly pro-war and didn't mind telling me so. The fact that these working class, Irish Catholic boys were much more likely to fight and die in Vietnam than I or my college classmates, wasn't lost on me entirely and kept me from bringing up the subject with them.

After graduation I joined the Federal government's VISTA program— then known informally as a domestic Peace Corps. To many, these agencies symbolized a kind of political and social idealism. To General Curtis LeMay, then the Director of the Selective Service System and a strong supporter of VISTA and the Peace Corps, they were identical twins. Both "channeled" young people who opposed the war to places where they could be less effective protestors. This was certainly true in my case.

I worked for two years in a large prison on Riker's Island in New York City. Among the memories I have from working on Riker's and living in our "target population's" neighborhood in the South Bronx, I still vividly remember passing long lines of inmates moving slowly in the opposite direction through the prison corridors. Sometimes they would ask me to get them a court date; usually they just teased me about my long hair. It didn't matter whether I was tutoring small groups of inmates in the prison library, discussing future job training programs with them individually, or just relaying information to them from their mothers. They casually described the pervasive violence in their lives on the street and in prison—liberally mixing fact and fiction. It was still a game to them, and that scared me.

After VISTA, I stayed in the South Bronx and worked for another year with the Bronx Legal Aid Society. With the help of two Legal Aids, I put together a small court diversion project for teenage boys charged with misdemeanors and held in the juvenile detention center on Riker's. I would talk to them in the overcrowded holding pen inside the old courthouse on 163rd Street and Third Avenue before arraignment, and then again on Riker's. They almost never made bail, so a few months after arraignment I would approach the judge in chambers with a plea bargain that the assistant District Attorney and the Legal Aid were ready to accept.

Nothing had prepared me for this world in which plea bargaining made actual guilt and innocence irrelevant. Yet, as long as I spoke with humility, did some simple background checks, made a few phone calls to drug treatment programs, and acknowledged that the work we did was futile, everyone was willing to trust me. That was as frightening, I realized, as the time I spent in prison. It shocked me that I could have any influence on the legal process, and especially because the judges and attorneys were in such a state of confusion and held the law in such low esteem. Most of all, it scared me that our clients, 17- and 18-year-old African-American and Puerto Rican boys with little education or chance for a job, and their families could see exactly what I could see and were helpless to do anything about it.

During this period in my life I briefly considered going to law school, but since I already had lasted longer than most of the attorneys who started with me at Legal Aid, this didn't seem like a very promising career move. Instead, I went to graduate school to study political philosophy. I thought that perhaps there was a way to bring these unnerving experiences under one theoretical roof.

After two years in graduate school, where I took advantage of my courtroom skills to elbow my way to the front of the class, I moved back to the Bronx to write my dissertation, work as a part-time teacher in an adult literacy program, and help my future wife's community-based political theater company when I could. Gradually, my academic interests turned from the abstract topics of justice and equality to a more concrete concern with democratic political education. How, I wondered, can those most alienated from our political society acquire the skills and habits needed to make their voices heard?

I also began to think about possible connections between the Johnson Administration's "war on poverty" that had made it possible for me to see up close a side of life I had never imagined and the expanding war in Southeast Asia that I had repeatedly imagined from afar. In what sense, I wondered, was poverty a form of violence? If it was violence, was the "war on poverty" a kind of counter-violence designed to defeat the violence of poverty? Similarly, was violent protest against an unjust war in Southeast Asia violent in the same way that the war itself was violent? If I could only define violence in general, I thought, perhaps all of these pieces would fall into place.

Today, I no longer believe that a general theory of violence is possible. But even if it is possible, I don't think this is what students need in order to come to terms with the shocks I experienced after college and that they are likely to encounter at some point in their lives. The course on war and morality and the service-learning option described in this essay are moti-

vated by a hope that political philosophy can help students see the relationships between various forms of *political* violence. Not surprisingly, these
were not the hopes and goals of my students when the course began.

On the first day of class, a student asked, "Why should I take this
course? I'm a senior, and this course has nothing to do with my major. I
could probably take another general education course that would fulfill the
graduation requirement that landed me in this class, and that would have
less reading and less writing than this one." I was stunned, although I probably should not have been. Like most colleges and universities, Michigan
State University now makes it clear to its students that they and their families are consumers who deserve a good product at a reasonable price. This
student was only expressing what was on the minds of most of the other
students in the class: "This better be a good deal."

I responded, not very eloquently, that even though she did not think
the experiences of war that citizens have endured on, behind, and between
the battle lines have much to do with her major or her life right now, that
will probably change. I said that it is likely that war will touch her in one
way or another, at some time or another. It may not even be the result of a
new unforeseen war. Someday she may find herself trying to comfort a parent, grandparent, or someone else close to her who needs help coming to
terms with the memories of war and its aftermath. It is better to think
about these things before they happen. In the rush of events it is much
harder to sort things out, and even if we can sort them out, it is hard to do
the right thing without some forethought.

Another student then asked, "Have you fought in any wars?" My
mind began to race. I began by telling the class that I lived through several
wars that the United States had been involved in, beginning with Vietnam
but including the wars in Central America during the 1980s and the Persian

Gulf War. I alluded to my opposition to these wars, but then, as a counter-point, I mentioned that many of my relatives were deeply involved in World War II and that their experiences and losses also had been important in shaping my views about war and peace.

The second student sat expressionless. Then, he asked, "Is this a course about war or about anti-war protests?" That first-day-of-class fear was never higher than it was at this moment. I wasn't just afraid that I wouldn't capture their attention or they wouldn't like me. I was afraid that they were seeing right through me. The same insecurity and fear that had swept over me when looking into the skeptical eyes of defendants who knew all too well what a cynical business the criminal justice system is rushed back. Here I was again, staring into disbelieving eyes without a leg to stand on and no one to bail me out.

But, before I finish this story, let me explain more carefully what I mean by the responsibility of political philosophers to teach students how to come to terms with political violence.

POLITICAL RESPONSIBILITY

In a recent article on service-learning that appeared in the September 1997 issue of *Teaching Philosophy,* Patrick Fitzgerald argues that it is ironic that moral philosophers do not include themselves when reminding professionals of their broad social responsibilities and specific moral duties to their patients and clients. Philosophers are professionals too, yet they rarely worry about what they owe society in return for their privileged position.

Fitzgerald suggests that one way that moral philosophers who teach applied ethics can meet their own social responsibility is through service-learning options in their courses. The main benefit to students and society from this kind of service is that students seem to be better prepared for and more likely to perform socially responsible activities later on. At least, that is what the students in Fitzgerald's small sample said. After performing their public service, they believed that they were more understanding of the sick and unfortunate and more likely to lend a helping hand. Leaving aside the reliability of this self-assessment, are there similar responsibilities and potential benefits for philosophers who teach political philosophy, not applied ethics?

The first thing to note is an important difference between courses in political philosophy and applied ethics. Whereas applied ethics courses aim to prepare professionals to act morally, the standard political philosophy courses do not have the same kind of normative developmental purpose. Applied ethics courses emphasize the positive responsibilities of professionals, including the duty to respect the rights of patients and clients. Although some political philosophers, including John Rawls in *A Theory of Justice,* have discussed the noblesse oblige of public administrators, most political philosophy does not distinguish between professional and civic responsibilities. In a democratic society all citizens, including political philosophers, have a strong but qualified allegiance to the state and a duty to respect the rights of their fellow citizens. Academic political philosophers explain, justify, and sometimes criticize this allegiance and these rights and duties.

This difference in purpose is reflected in a difference in content between applied ethics and political philosophy courses. The sub-field of applied ethics in moral philosophy continues to grow rapidly. From its origins in medical and legal ethics, it now has a foothold in almost every professional discipline from engineering and architecture to business and journalism. The format of applied ethics courses across the board is roughly the same. Students are confronted with moral dilemmas and given a choice of methods for resolving them. Some methods, like utilitarianism, are fairly abstract. Sometimes it is more casuistic and tailored to the particular problems faced by the profession in question. In any case, applied ethics courses follow a fairly predictable trajectory from contemporary problems as different as brain death and the risk of a suspension bridge collapsing to moral judgments and back again.

In contrast, political philosophy courses, whether taught in philosophy departments or under the name political theory in political science departments, focus on the structure and limits of government that can make it a legitimate object of political loyalty. Some political philosophy courses are historical, concentrating on the structure of government in texts such as Plato's *Republic* or Hegel's *Philosophy of Right*. Other political philosophy courses are organized around problems or topics such as justice, political equality, and freedom of speech through the writings of contemporary philosophers such as John Rawls, Martha Nussbaum, and Ronald Dworkin. Instead of emphasizing the legitimacy of government, they focus on the rights a legitimate government should protect and the duties its citizens have when their rights are protected.

Neither historical nor problems courses in political philosophy are addressed to future politicians or public policy makers. They are addressed to citizens and designed to teach greater political literacy, that is, how to speak the language of rights and duties. Even though many pre-law undergraduates take these and other philosophy courses, they do so usually because they have heard that they will help them score well on the LSAT, not because they think political philosophy will make them more politically responsible lawyers or public officials.

In political philosophy courses like these, what should students learn that is analogous to the moral character development that Fitzgerald claims service-learning can provide in applied ethics courses? One answer is that they should learn about the limits of political obligation, even in a just or well-ordered society. This seems too narrow to me. It reduces political responsibility to the occasional crisis when politics intrudes into everyday life and no longer can be ignored. My preference, no doubt a product of my own political education, is that political philosophy should enable students to recognize the origins, forms, and effects of violence in the political society they inhabit, so that they may be able to limit and cope with political violence before civil disobedience becomes the only alternative to uncritical acquiescence or complicity.

SERVICE-LEARNING

The 200 students in my general education course on war and morality in spring 1998 were assigned J. Glenn Gray's *The Warriors,* Tim O'Brien's *The Things They Carried,* and Robert Kotlowitz's *Before Their Time*—plus selections from *Monkey Bridge* by Lan Cao, *The Good War* by Studs Terkel, James Carroll's *An American Requiem,* Paul Hendrickson's *The Living and the Dead,* and *Fragments* by Binjamin Wilkomirski. They also read more theoretical essays by Martin Luther King, Jr. and Michael Walzer. I tried not to point the course toward any one moral lesson—either pro-war or anti-war. There was, however, an underlying assumption that I took from Gray: how we remember and represent the profound experiences of war likely will affect how well we come to terms with violence in this and other forms later in our lives. Sometimes, as Hannah Arendt has said, acts of immense violence can be thoughtless, almost banal. Other times, the violence can be mesmerizing, almost ecstatic. Between these two extremes is a large range of wartime experience that needs careful, fine-grained description and interpretation.

Although I have taught this course twice before, this is the first time that I offered a service-learning option. The service-learning option was a collaborative writing project that had several parts. Twenty individual students were paired up with twenty community volunteers for approximately two hours per week during ten out of the fifteen weeks. The student's main task was to produce a written account of the volunteer's wartime experience. The experience could have been in combat as a soldier, nurse, or doctor; behind the lines as a parent, loved one, or industrial worker; or between the lines as a prisoner of war, a refugee or a war protestor. One goal of this part of the project was to get the student and community volunteer to work on something that would be of mutual benefit to them. The student would benefit from learning firsthand how difficult it is to come to terms with the experience of war. The volunteer would receive assistance putting this experience into words, thereby gaining greater control over it. A second goal was to get the students to stand back and reflect on the relationship between the wartime story they helped compose and the other material they read for the course. In addition to the collaborative writing project, the students wrote a three-to-five-page interpretive essay relating these two things. Which books and articles they used depended upon the content of the wartime story they helped their community volunteer to write.

An additional task for students in the service-learning project was to meet in small groups with me to discuss how their collaborative writing project was going. I met with the students three times in groups of four to nine students. Some students had problems getting started, especially where their community volunteer was elderly and had a difficult time focusing on a single incident or set of experiences. Other students had no trouble at all and hit it off with their community volunteer right away.

These small group discussions were awkward at first. The students were nervous about the project and nervous about how I was going to grade them on it. For some this remained true throughout the semester. But most of them soon came to enjoy reporting to the group on the unexpected obstacles they encountered and the curious things they learned from their community volunteer. "I got an idea of what ideas others had for the final project, what kinds of questions to ask my volunteer." Another felt relief: "It made me realize that I wasn't the only one having minor problems. Also, I felt good because many had more difficulty."

The final task was to turn the wartime stories into a script for a readers theater performed by three students from the theater department. This was performed at the end of the semester for all of the students in the class and the community volunteers, almost all of whom came, some with their families. The idea here, in addition to recognizing publicly the work of the students and the community volunteers, was to bring the service-learning project back to the class as a whole so that other students could learn from it as well. As one student said, "The best part was seeing the faces of the volunteers light up—everything was worth it. This also served as a benefit to those students who didn't partake in this option, I'm sure." Unfortunately, of the roughly 150 other students in the class who completed a course evaluation at the end of the semester, no one commented on the readers theater with this much enthusiasm.

After the readers theater, I collected the wartime stories in a small 30-page booklet that was given to the service-learning students at the final examination and mailed to all of the community volunteers. The service-learning students also filled out a short evaluation of the service-learning option in addition to the regular course evaluation that all of the students in the course completed. Students thought the project was "wonderful" and "an experience to remember." Slightly more revealing were comments about "actually seeing" how war affects veterans, not just reading about it, and how the books we read themselves "became more real." Only in casual conversations with a few students after the semester was over was I able to gauge just how powerfully the project had affected them. For example, one student proudly showed me a picture of her and her roommates celebrating her community volunteer's birthday at the volunteer's home.

Finally, I solicited by mail evaluative comments from the community volunteers. Not all responded, but those that did expressed both appreciation for the opportunity to get to know their student on a personal level and satisfaction with the way that they were able to make a little more sense of their own wartime experience. The community volunteers tended to take more time composing their evaluations than the students did. Several spoke about the importance of the project and the readers theater for their families. As one said, "I learned something about articulating my memories of war—I hadn't done much of this, especially with my own family members." For another, "It was cathartic, but also allowed me to write it down for my own family, and now put it behind me." One community volunteer said "I have grandchildren and great grandchildren who could never understand. It is difficult to convey your true feelings about wartime experiences."

These comments surprised me. I did not expect that the project would enable the community volunteers to rethink and publicly present experiences that they had not shared with their own family members at all. I thought that the volunteers would be people who already felt very comfortable sharing their stories. For some, it seems, this public remembering could now take the place of sharing these memories with their families. For others, it may serve as a first chapter in a new conversation with their children and grandchildren.

In general, the comments that the service-learning students made about the course, consistent with their interpretive essays, suggest that they felt that they did learn something about wartime experience that they did not get from the other readings and the classroom discussions in the course. It is difficult, however, to say exactly what this is. Almost all of them personally connected with their community volunteers, and said that just meeting someone with this kind of rich story to tell and helping them tell it was moving for them. Some were more articulate than others in identifying parallels between episodes in the books they read and the wartime stories of their volunteers. This was the subject of their interpretive essay and the quality of these varied considerably.

On the negative side, some service-learning students felt that the amount of work they put into the project was not reflected adequately in the formula for calculating the final course grade. Other students who did not participate in the service-learning project felt that service-learning students were graded on a more generous scale than they were. In fact, the grades for the service-learning students were slightly higher than for the rest of the class. My teaching assistants gently reminded me of this at the end of the semester, and I am sure that I had more to do with this than I should have. One could argue that the service-learning students chose this project because they knew that their learning styles were more suited to this kind of work than the standard academic paper assignment. There is probably some truth to this. My impression, when I visited regular recitation sections late in the semester, was that some of the service-learning students who had received relatively high grades on their interpretive essays were not contributing as well to the recitation section as most of the other students, yet on average they received a higher grade for the course.

None of the students said in the service-learning evaluation that he or she saw political violence in his or her own life more clearly. It hardly occurred to them. What does come through is a new confidence in their ability to make sense of experiences radically different from their own. "It made me see things from a different perspective. Very satisfying." From the perspective of a Vietnam Vet who was "infuriated at the mass media"? From the perspective of a World War II Navy WAVE who defended her daughter when she was "involved in sitdowns during high school to protest Vietnam"? From the perspective of a pacifist serving as a medic in World War II who "realized then that he needed and wanted to join the fighting force"? From the perspective of a Navy Task Force Commander in Vietnam who refused to obey a superior's foolish order "to send his men out to ambush every night"? The students working with these community volunteers knew that something was up. They knew that the bright line between violence and legitimate force had been blurred in these cases, even though they didn't label it political violence.

One of our authors, Robert Kotlowitz, visited the class to read from his World War II memoir and take questions. In response to one student who asked "What did you learn from your wartime experience?" he said, " I learned that I am both much less and much more than I thought I was before I went to war." Kotlowitz, one of three survivors in a group of 40 soldiers killed in an obscure battle in France, does not fit the stereotype of the battlefield hero. On his return to camp, after he was pinned down for 12 hours in the mud by enemy machine gun fire and had to listen to the other soldiers slowly die around him, he tried to confront the officers responsible for ordering this suicidal mission. He could only recoil in disgust at their feeble attempts to deny their responsibility for this tragedy. "They couldn't wait to get rid of me," he said.

That Kotlowitz, a private drafted into the war right out of college, has come to terms with this single act of political violence forty years later suggests it may be too early to assess the effect of this service-learning experience. A better measure of the success of service-learning projects such as this may be whether later in life students can recognize political violence when they see it. It takes a long time to build the kind of public spiritedness that democratic citizens need to handle political violence in their own lives. Learning to come to terms with violence in a democratic way is, indeed, a long haul.

Through *Grand Canyon* and Eastern Europe to *Habits of the Heart:* A Professor's Journey

Myron A. Levine

In *Habits of the Heart,* one of the most influential books of recent years, Robert Bellah and his colleagues point to the eroding sense of community and connectedness in the contemporary United States. American individualism, both material and expressive, has triumphed over long-standing, countervailing religious and civic traditions. Americans today define success in highly individualistic, shallow terms, not, as they did a century ago, in terms, as Bellah puts it, "of the conventions of one's local community." Career choices today often reflect a desire for material and expressive satisfaction rather than the pursuit of a "calling"—a word that to our ears today sounds terribly quaint and old-fashioned. Americans have drifted from Bellah's faith that "a self worth having only comes into existence

through participation with others in the effort to create a just and loving society."

Exaggerated individualism has led to feelings of insecurity and isolation. Americans have sought intimacy in insular suburbs and other segmented "lifestyle enclaves" that celebrate "the narcissism of similarity." As Bellah quite correctly observes, associations based on shared lifestyles and the protection of privilege are poor substitutes for a full, rich, and authentic community that embraces and values diversity and change. Bellah's solution is to propose a highly utopian transformation of American life based on the revival of America's "second language" of moral commitment, communal traditions, and spirituality, a language of obligation and shared fate that can help counterbalance the "first language" of individualism.

I am among those college professors whose outlook and teaching have greatly been influenced by *Habits*. Yet it was not a perspective that came to me easily. When I initially read *Habits*, I rejected much of its perspective as conservative, apolitical, unrealistic, and naïve. As I shall discuss further at the end of this essay, I still maintain differences with Bellah in a number of important areas. I am a political scientist who, schooled in the 1960s, continues to see the importance of conflict—and at times even threat—in bringing about progressive change to improve the conditions of America's "have nots." Yet, over the years, I have increasingly come around to Bellah's orientation. He and his co-authors have convinced me that there is no need to rely on conflict strategies, that productive change can quite often be brought about through more consensual strategies that seek to increase people's understanding of what they, as human beings and members of a community, share in common. Where possible, strategic choices must represent a respect for each individual's human dignity, a respect that is not accorded in disintegrative conflict and violence.

Over the years, I have come to believe in the importance of introducing students to Bellah's observations concerning individualism, community, and obligation. But I have found that students often have great difficulty with the text itself; except for the initial chapter, they do not find it an easy book to read. As a result, I have tried to find other vehicles, in addition to the book itself, to introduce the idea of community in the classroom.

As a result, in courses where I discuss "community," I often use a very beautiful and thought-provoking film, *Grand Canyon.* But even here, as I shall discuss in some detail, I have found that students, mired in the first language of individualism, have a difficult time grasping the communal and spiritual themes of this very serious film.

Of course, I am not the only teacher who has seen the importance of having students confront Bellah's book and their rugged individualism. In *The Courage to Teach,* Parker Palmer reports his own frustrations as he finds that his students too easily accept Bellah's description of American individualism as an accurate portrayal of their own lives. "Most of them," Palmer notes, "said the same thing: they wanted 'freedom from' things like unhealthy family ties, narrow religious beliefs, and prejudiced communities, and they wanted 'freedom to' be themselves, choose for themselves, express themselves, and even 'be selfish.'" Even after a very extensive discussion of *Habits,* his students still remain so blinded by individualism that they fail to see how their own lives have been shaped by important (albeit often unrecognized) communal values and traditions that help to offset the excesses of individualism. Although they have read Bellah's text, they have not been able to use it to explore the potential of, as well as the limits of, "self."

Palmer is the rare teacher who will not let such a situation stand. When one of the students, a young man of religious faith and humane spirit, tells the group a humorous story of how he was falsely arrested for drug-dealing in what turned out to be a case of mistaken identity, Palmer sees the opportunity for a teaching moment and asks: "Why didn't you sue the police for false arrest? You might have gotten rich overnight?" The student responds that he was just glad the case of mistaken identity was cleared up. Palmer continues:

> Then, defending and excusing the police, he said, 'Everyone makes mistakes.' Almost all the other students quickly made it clear that they agreed with his moral position. I pursued the inquiry: 'Let me hold a mirror up to you. You talk in terms of individualism and self-seeking, but underneath all of that you have such a strong sense of communal membership that you are willing to forgive the police their mistake rather than try to make money off it. The kind of individualism the authors of *Habits* are talking about is not softened by that sense of community. The stereotypical individualist would have hired a lawyer that evening and filed suit the next morning.'

In effect, Palmer the teacher has enabled students to use the "little stories" of their lives to "check and correct the big story" presented by Bellah.

Why have I moved and become increasingly positive in embracing inclusive strategies and seeing the harm inherent in conflict strategies? In part, my own transformation may to some extent simply be the result of age and family responsibilities which oftentimes brings with it a fear of destructive change. But my transformation is also the result of my own learning, a result of my having learned a new field, and with it, having come to understood the power and importance of developing a civil society.

Although I am primarily an Americanist and urbanist, in recent years I have had a number of opportunities to travel in, and teach about, Eastern and Central Europe. In reading about the changes that have been brought to that part of the world, I am awed by the achievements of such political dissidents as Vaclav Havel, who later became the president of the Czech Republic. These dissidents succeeded in doing the impossible: they brought down a totalitarian system and did so (except in Romania and Yugoslavia) through a bloodless "Velvet Revolution" that avoided the tragic human costs of a more violent revolution. The 1989 revolution in Eastern and Central Europe underscores a major point in the writings not just of Bellah but of Alexis de Tocqueville: the "habits of the heart" that sustain democracy, the empathy and participatory skills necessary for the institutionalization of civil society, are developed through associational memberships and interpersonal interactions in community and religious organizations.

As I noted before, I have not totally shaken off my 1960s' perspective, and, consequently, I can still be quite critical in pointing to the limitations of the strategies of Vaclav Havel and Martin Luther King, Jr., even while I celebrate the great achievements of these leaders and their vision and strategy. Indeed, Havel himself has come to recognize the situational limits of his vision of a partyless, apolitical politics of the state. Havel freely confesses that his great failures as president were at least partly due to his refusal to form a conventional political party after the 1989 revolution. Havel believed that he could transform politics and human nature; he sought a "revolutionary" politics that would promote the public interest and surmount the narrowness and divisiveness of parties. Yet, his unwillingness to convert the umbrella, anti-communist Civic Forum movement into a post-1989 political party only served to allow his more market-oriented opponents to form a party of their own and win control of the new Czech government. The results were the enactment of policies that slighted Havel's more humanistic values and aggravated relationships between the Czech and

Slovak regions of the country, leading to the country's peaceful break-up or "Velvet Divorce."

I would now like to have the reader accompany me on a brief journey through the film *Grand Canyon* and Eastern Europe to *Habits of the Heart* as I further describe my efforts to come to grips with the tensions imposed by individualism and community in American life and the potential for change inherent in strategies based on community and consensus as opposed to opposition and conflict.

There is perhaps no more capable visual presentation of Bellah's powerful themes than Lawrence and Meg Kasdan's film *Grand Canyon,* produced in 1991. With a stunning cast that includes Kevin Kline, Danny Glover, and Steve Martin, among others, the movie uses contemporary Los Angeles as the metaphor for modern American ills. It is a film about the lack of connectedness in American life, the shallowness of life in suburban enclaves, and the inability of careerism and material wealth to provide a life of meaning. It is a serious film, a film that Lawrence Kasdan, interviewed in the late 1990s, said can no longer be made in Hollywood.

Grand Canyon starts with a particularly dramatic warning of the dire consequences that await as a result of our failure to establish genuine communities. Suburban and yuppified America lives a life of comfort, wealth, and privilege in its secure and insular enclave. However, the potential for violence exists when members of the fragmented American landscape cross paths.

Mack (Kevin Kline), tired of sitting in traffic after a Lakers' game, seeks an alternative route through inner-city Los Angeles. His car breaks down, and his cellular phone battery winds down. He finds himself in the wrong neighborhood at the mercy of a gang whose leader demands that he get out of the car. He is saved only by the sudden arrival of an African

American tow-truck driver, Simon (Danny Glover), who intercedes with the gang leader. The incident motivates Mack to reach beyond his safe suburban existence into someone else's life. He seeks to repay Simon by finding an apartment for his sister and her family who are being terrorized by inner-city gang violence. Mack even arranges a date for Simon, a widower, with a black co-worker, and love blooms. By the end of the picture, Mack has moved beyond the isolation and general sense of unease with his life. He and his wife adopt an abandoned Hispanic baby girl (as his wife had wanted), and he establishes a genuine friendship with Simon.

Despite his material success and the helping nature of his work as an immigration attorney, Mack, when we first see him, is bored with his life. He is suffering anomie. Unsatisfied with his career, he enters into a brief, passionless liaison with his young legal assistant, Dee (Mary-Louise Parker). Despite his infidelity, Mack, who cares about his wife and their son, is portrayed as a troubled but admirable figure when compared to some of the other main characters in the film.

Mack's friend, Davis (Steve Martin), is a big-money producer of particularly gory blood-and-guts action films. Davis stands for the excesses of American individualism, resisting any sense of obligation to community. He pleads artistic freedom and refuses to trim even the most disgusting and violent cinematic shots. Davis is a shallow figure, trapped by the seductions of materialism and career success, and unable to enter into any meaningful human attachments outside of his friendship with Mack. He is insensitive to the cries of his girlfriend (of course, a very attractive, younger woman) who pleads to have a baby as her biological time clock ticks away. He cannot even recognize that genuine service and caring can be freely given and are often their own reward.

Even a robbery and gunshot wound to the knee, which leaves Davis partially crippled, only results in a momentary spiritual reawakening and a promise to undertake only life-affirming work—a shallow commitment he quickly recants. He is soon back at work turning out more films of graphic violence and eyeing pretty women on the studio lot. He takes a professional's pride in the films he turns out and the entertainment and escapism that these films provide.

While Davis is in many ways shallow and despicable, he certainly is not the most pathetic character in the film. Mack's young legal assistant, Dee, is desperately unhappy with life. She is longing for love and a meaningful relationship and, in almost predatory fashion, pursues the affections of Mack. Dee even resents it when her co-worker and office friend, Jane (Alfre Woodard) falls in love with Simon as a result of Mack's intervention. Dee is desperately lost and egocentric; it should have been her who found love! Her job and career do not bring happiness or any satisfaction at all. Her sense of solitariness and frustration are further visualized in a dream sequence where Mack flies between the office towers of Los Angeles, looks into the window of Dee's apartment and sees her tossing fitfully, alone in her bed.

The only good characters in the film are those who recognize their connectedness with others—despite the repeated caution of Simon that there are limits, that you just can't intrude in and "mess" with the lives of others (an admonition from which Simon retreats by the end of the film). Simon is almost saint-like in his caring for his sister's family, his deaf daughter, and in his intervention to save Mack, a white stranger.

Mack's wife, Claire (Mary McDonnell), is the film's other main caring character. But now that their son Roberto is nearly grown, she is suffering from an empty-nest syndrome; she too, is bored with her suburban life despite the success of her career and the home she has built. She does voluntary work; she cares for others. She will not permit herself to choose a jogging path that will allow her to look away from the homeless sleeping in the alley in her otherwise prosperous suburb. She has a spiritual side and is looking for something larger. She believes that miracles are happening every day, but that people refuse to recognize them.

Other admirable characters in the film include Roberto and his girlfriend, young people who are portrayed as the hope of the future. They are counselors in a summer camp who treat children with genuine care and understanding. They are also developing a genuine sense of affection for each other.

Grand Canyon is blatantly a spiritual film, as *Washington Post* writer Joe Brown underscores in a January 10, 1992 review. "Pervading the film is a distinctly metaphysical (or new age, if you must) question about the nature of the impulses and coincidences (miracles?) that set these stalled characters moving again. The continually circling surveillance helicopters that hover over nearly every scene can be viewed as ominous, but may also be seen as guardian angels." The Grand Canyon in Arizona is itself obviously a metaphor for the deep divisions that keep us—and our communities—separate from one another. But the metaphor implies still more. In the film's closing-scene visit to the Grand Canyon, the characters express their awe standing before a creation that shows a work or design much larger than their lives. Indeed, our lives pale in significance when compared to the majesty of the Grand Canyon and the time and power—the spiritual force—that it embodies. As Simon tries to explain his seemingly chance friendship with Mack and his falling in love with Jane, maybe, just maybe, everything is put on Earth for a reason.

The intervention of larger, spiritual forces dominate key moments in the lives of the film's major characters. The intervention of these forces, however, does not lend itself to rational explanation. Mack remembers the mystical experience of how he was pulled back onto the curb and prevented from walking under a bus by a women who magically appeared "out of nowhere" wearing the hat of his favorite baseball team—and then disappeared again. What would a woman with a Pittsburgh Pirates cap be doing in Los Angeles? Mack's wife, Claire, feels that she did not just happen to jog by an abandoned infant by accident; rather, some larger force seemingly pulled her to the child lying deep in the bushes. Claire argues with Mack that there are miracles every day, but we just do not recognize them anymore. There is also a mystical, almost Jesus-like homeless person who seems to magically appear and disappear in this otherwise prosperous suburb. Claire jogs by, and the stranger, in his delirium (or is it a religious-like chant?), seemingly tells her, in her moment of doubt, to keep the baby. This mystical stranger, too, appears to be the agent of a larger force that guides and shapes our lives.

I have used *Grand Canyon* as a regular part of the curriculum in my Albion College "Community, Voluntarism and Citizenship" class and a special week-long program that I host each year for 100 college-bound high school juniors. In part, students gain admission to this latter program on the basis of their records of school and community service. Nonetheless, the film often puzzles students. For the younger students, it is often the first serious film they have seen, and they need a good deal of pre-film preparation and post-film discussion and debriefing for the film to make sense. With the preparation and a good deal of discussion, the film receives overwhelming positive student reviews (despite the fact that it is about a half hour too long and that the hokey dream sequence in the film just does not work).

One year a family health emergency kept me from "prepping" the high school students in advance of the film. I was, however, able to be there for a discussion the day after the film was shown. I asked them what they thought of the film. The students (or at least those who spoke) universally disliked it. It was "boring." "I couldn't see the point." "It had no plot." "It had no conclusion."

In part, these students have the contemporary culture of expressive individualism so imbedded in them that they could not relate to a movie constructed around Bellah's "second language" of community and responsibility. The students have special difficulty relating to the scenes that discuss spiritual forces and visions. They laugh and giggle at the dream sequence of Mack flying through the L.A. night observing the miseries of others (a scene that actually merits some derision as it is badly crafted and seemingly out of place in the film).

These young students have not yet learned to take film—not just the Kasdans' substantive message—seriously. They relate to movies only in terms of expressive individualism. Movies are mass entertainment, mass action vehicles designed for their pleasure and immediate gratification, where they are treated as objects to be manipulated rather than active participants in a film-centered discourse. They have not been taught to view a film as a meaningful statement of the human condition and a means to dialogue—a vehicle through which the audience is prompted to reflect on the meaning of life and its difficulties. Students have especially great difficulty in relating to the film's spiritual themes. Kasdan preaches a message of spiritual possibility that is working against what today's more cynical and individualist-absorbed youth audience is often able to see. Students have to be introduced to Bellah's "second language" before they can see the merit in the film.

As I have already noted, my scholarly interests are not confined solely to American politics. I have taught in Eastern Europe—in the former

Yugoslavia and more recently in the Czech Republic and Latvia. On occasion, I teach a course on Political Change in Eastern Europe. As I have confronted the works of Vaclav Havel and other East European former dissidents and intellectuals, I have gained a new appreciation for the importance of "antipolitics" and of building a "civil society" distinct from government. Havel, like Bellah, argues for a politics of the public good that moves beyond conceptualizations of politics as mere pluralist interplay. A "moral politics" can be transformative. But as the story of Czech President Vaclav Havel shows, the notion of a "moral politics" can also at times prove to be highly unrealistic and self-defeating.

The communist era destroyed (or severely weakened) many of the institutions necessary for a civil society. Communism sought to eliminate or control the voices of churches, trade unions, and other ethnic and voluntary associations. Communism also obliterated a sense that participation in public life is virtuous. Indeed, politics in the post-communist nations of Europe may still suffer from what Ken Jowitt has called a "Leninist legacy," where citizens persist in the engrained communist-era attitude of disdaining all participation in public life as inherently corrupting.

It was the response of political dissidents to the corrupting influence of public life under communism that especially piqued my interest. Under the communist regimes, any participant in public life—even an artist—had to sacrifice his or her authenticity and give public recognition of fealty to the officially approved platitudes. As then-dissident playwright Vaclav Havel eloquently phrased it in his classic essay "The Power of the Powerless," involvement in public life under communism forced one to "live within a lie" as opposed to "living in truth." Havel describes the debilitating corruption of the human spirit that occurs when a person is forced to sacrifice authenticity.

Under late communism, even government officials could no longer believe the official lies and stories and dogma of the communist regime. No longer motivated by ideological fervor, involvement in public life became simply a matter of self-interest—the pursuit of special privileges and favors (and the desire to avoid punishments and repression), nothing more. The system ossified as the human spirit stultified.

Many dissidents sought to avoid spiritual corruption by retreating to the relative safety of "antipolitics." They were involved in artistic ventures, "green" environmental groups, and other actions that promoted human values but were not seen as overtly political or as posing a direct threat to communist rule. Their actions would help to carve out an incipient public space—free from direct state control—that others would later expand.

According to Havel, the good human being has no choice but to participate in public life and witness against an immoral regime. To avoid the corrupting influences of public life, however, such participation can only be done on a moral basis. For Havel, a moral politics transcends individual and group interest and instead represents the pursuit of the public good, the good of the nation. As Vladimir Tismaneanu has observed in his 1992 book *Reinventing Politics: Eastern Europe from Stalin to Havel,* Havel rejected a politics of pluralism based only on self-interest and ideology. Instead, he sought public action based on universal moral values and the free exercise of an individual's basic rights.

Sure of the moral correctness of their position, Havel and other dissidents were able to withstand the jail sentences and other punishments meted out by the communists. Their idealistic, principled action proved transformative and in 1992 resulted in a virtually bloodless Velvet Revolution that pulled down the communist regime.

Havel sought to bring a new moral politics to the new Czechoslovakia. He disdained forming a political party as he thought that parties divided the nation and led party members to look at public life narrowly in terms of their partisan self-interest; he feared the excessive influence of parties, what, in *Summer Meditations*, he called "the dictatorship of partisanship." For Havel, political parties were only one of a vast variety of organizations, movements, clubs, and unions that would flower in civil society. Havel believed that true democracy entailed more than just party activity, a clash of ideologies, and elections. Instead, Havel saw it as his responsibility to emphasize "the moral origins of all genuine politics, to stress the significance of moral values and standards in all spheres of social life . . . and to rediscover or cultivate . . . 'higher responsibility.'"

As President of the newly freed nation, Havel's politics-as-morality vision soon confronted hard reality, and he suffered a number of severe disappointments. Havel had hoped that the revolutionary umbrella organization Civic Forum would continue to govern the country in a welcome-all-groups fashion. But while Havel refused to form a political party, other Czech leaders did, and the country fractionalized politically. Havel was acclaimed president, but Vaclav Klaus, the country's finance minister, took control of Civic Forum, converting it into a political party with a conservative free-market platform that was inconsistent with many of the social justice tenets of Havel's moral politics. For Havel, the doctrinaire pursuit of a free market could be just as much as confining an ideology as communism; unabridged free markets do not provide for governmental action to protect both the nation's heritage and the dignity of the individual.

The break-up of Czechoslovakia into two separate nations was Havel's greatest disappointment as President. Despite his efforts to mute tensions, Czech and Slovak political leaders pursued their separate interests, exaggerating the grievances that eventually produced a peaceful Velvet Divorce. Slovak politicos even resented Havel's efforts at mediation, portraying the

Czech president as a "sly oppressor" attempting to do little more than maintain the status quo and Czech hegemony.

Havel's disappointments attest to the limitations of the moral vision when faced with the self-interest of real-world politicians and parochial ethnic constituencies. But the limitations of Havel's moral politics should not blind us to the amazing successes achieved by his politics based on moral vision and the public interest. Even during the communist era, a number of anticommunist critics charged that Havel and other dissidents were unrealistic idealists whose protests would accomplish little other than bringing about their own internment. Nonetheless, Havel and other dissidents did the seeming impossible; they provided the moral example that paved the way for the mass mobilization that brought down communism. Like water dripping on a rock, their actions eventually cracked the rock. Havel's politics succeeded in changing an entire political system. But as President, he could not fully triumph over rumor, ethnic antagonisms, and self interest. He was unable to transform the human spirit to the extent he desired.

Vaclav Havel, Poland's Adam Michnik, and other East European dissidents taught me the transformative potential of a moral politics that elevates the human spirit. Their vision is similar to that of Robert Bellah's "politics of the nation," a politics that transcends the mere pluralist interplay of conflicting group interests. In *Habits,* Bellah uses the civil rights movement as an example of politics of the nation. Bellah contrasts the success of the civil rights movement, its actions grounded in universal values and joint sisterhood/brotherhood, with the partiality and narrowness of the Black Power movement, an ideology that was not grounded in larger, universal values and which had a difficult time drawing political support outside the African American community.

The primarily white, middle-class student body of my classes easily—I would say "too easily"—shares Bellah's pejorative view of Black Power. Of course, most of my students have only a fragmentary and incomplete understanding of the 1960s. Throughout their school life, they have been taught to celebrate Martin Luther King, Jr., his strategy of nonviolence, and his attempts to reach out beyond the color line. Of course, most of them have little in-depth understanding of King's philosophy and the events that took place in the 1960s. They have little understanding of King's failures, where his tactics were unable to gain positive change. They have even less knowledge of Black Power, except, maybe, to feel that it was militant, divisive, and wrong.

But is Bellah totally correct in his observations? Are my students right in their agreement with Bellah's portrayal of the civil rights movement and Black Power? Just as Parker Palmer's students too quickly accepted Bellah's description of individualism as an accurate portrayal of their lives, my students too easily accept Bellah's laudatory treatment of the civil rights movement and his diminishment of Black Power. Even though Bellah is right in celebrating the universal values of the movement and the limited coalition-building prospects of Black Power, he too easily slights the victories of Black Power, achievements that were sometimes gained when more consensus-oriented strategies were stymied.

In fairness, it must be noted that Bellah's comments on racial politics do not occupy the center of his book. Still, he uses them to distinguish his preference for change strategies based on universal or shared values and a positive conceptualization of "justice" (the "politics of the nation") as opposed to strategies based only on power that seek only to advance a group's self interest (the "politics of pluralism"). Bellah criticizes Black Power for framing questions quite narrowly, in justifying action only in terms of raw power and a "me too" demand for group benefits without articulating a larger, more positive conceptualization of justice.

Bellah observes that by grounding its appeal in America's biblical and republican traditions, Martin Luther King, Jr.'s civil rights movement effected great change in the nation by appealing to values shared by whites and blacks alike. The actions of the movement were designed to draw the attention of the larger white community to the inconsistency between segregation and the community's professed religious faith and belief in the democratic creed. According to Bellah, however, the movement toward racial justice lost its "moral edge" when "black power" advocates abandoned universalism for a "special pleading" based only on group self-interest.

Bellah criticizes the narrowness and particularism of Black Power and other community action groups such as the California-based Campaign for Economic Democracy (CED), an organization dedicated to mobilizing the Hispanic poor. These groups, Bellah feels, know only what they are against and not what they are for. They lack a larger, positive, substantive vision of what constitutes a just or moral society. They advocate the empowerment of the poor, but Bellah asks "empowerment for what ends?" For Bellah, justice must be substantive, not just procedural. Public action must be preceded by dialogue that helps to refine a participant's virtue, to make him or her a better person. Newly empowered protest actors who have failed to refine their moral vision, Bellah maintains, are just as capable as their former oppressors of inflicting injury and injustice on others. Hence, Bellah admires "reflective" community groups where internal dialogue helps to advance each member's moral development beyond a concern just for securing immediate benefits. As he observes, "justice, not power, is the true end of politics." Bellah especially admires the civil rights movement with its roots in the black churches as it exhibited a respect for the dignity of every human being, a respect not at all accorded by the intimidation and threats of Black Power.

For Bellah, the stridency of Black Power rhetoric, the reliance of

Black Power on intimidating visual symbols (the raised fist and the gun), and Black Power's advocacy of separate development all helped to drive blacks and whites further apart, not to bring them together by achieving a recognition of what they, as G-d's children and citizens of the American tradition, share in common. Black Power even denied the value of racial integration.

Yet, while Bellah's argument is powerful, it seems to me that Bellah is mistaken on a number of counts. First of all, Black Power was not the abject failure that he implies. Black Power certainly divided America, and the confrontations that resulted could at times be quite ugly. But Black Power also achieved important and real results. It strengthened black pride, reinforced black cultural identity, and through direct organizing—at times backed up by an implicit threat of violence—secured new spending and social welfare commitments in the inner city.

Bellah also fails to recognize the Black Power evolved in response to the very real limitations of more conventional civil rights strategies. Despite his early successes, Martin Luther King, Jr.'s string of achievements effectively ran out when he reached cities, such as Albany, where politically savvy targets took the steps to avoid a confrontation that would cede to King the moral high ground. King did not succeed in every southern city. Nor did he achieve great success in the North, in fighting racial segregation and poverty in such cities as Chicago and suburban Cicero. In Chicago and elsewhere, many white Americans exhibited no unease in continuing to live in *de facto* segregated communities, despite King's efforts to reveal to them the inconsistency of segregation with their ethical, spiritual, and democratic teachings.

Bellah emphasizes civic dialogue and moral transformation. But it is not always necessary (sometimes it may even be impossible) to transform the human spirit in order to bring about equalizing change. A community group that limits its tactics in accordance with the dictates of the larger American republican and religious traditions may very well rule out those tactics that have the best chance of producing effective results. Even ties to established institutions with a history of pursuing social justice—churches and labor unions, as Bellah advocates—can at times prove to be a conservatizing force that narrows a community group's independence of action.

Bellah is further incorrect in implying that Black Power stalled America's progress on race. An alternative and more plausible explanation is that white America declares its rhetorical allegiance to the ideal of racial integration but then refuses to support those measures—plans for the racial balance of metropolitan schools, changes in land use and zoning ordinances to allow the placement of low-income housing in the suburbs, and targeted spending against poverty—that would truly bring about an integrated and more just society. It is white self-interest more than the self-interest and "special pleading" of Black Power that is the true culprit when it comes to explaining America's stalled progress on race.

Critical of Black Power, Bellah is similarly critical of affirmative action, a program that he also characterizes as group special pleading, a demand for particular benefits not justified by some larger, universal value scheme. Bellah fears that affirmative action has served to reinforce separation—group identities, group claims, and intergroup tensions. Yet, Bellah once again largely ignores the achievements of the particularistic strategy he condemns. Affirmative action has helped to build and incorporate a black middle class into the larger American society; group-based preferences have helped racial minorities—and women—gain access to education, public employment, and administrative and professional positions that they otherwise would have been denied.

In place of affirmative action, Bellah presents a broad outline of

actions for transforming American culture in order to bring about fundamental, redistributional social change. But, as he admits, this much-hoped-
for overhaul of the American culture is not likely to occur in the near and
not-so-near future. In comparison, it should be noted, the gains secured by
affirmative action are very real and are here in the present.

What Bellah fails to recognize is that a perfected pluralism, where
powerless groups gain the ability to represent their own points of view, may
in and of itself represent a "positive" vision of a fair, nonpaternalistic, and
"just" political system. If there is no easy way to identify the public interest,
the national interest, or the just society, perhaps the best we can seek is an
improved pluralism where every group has a seat at the bargaining table.
Improved pluralism definitely falls well short of Bellah's (and Havel's) ideal
of public action based on a substantive vision of justice. Nonetheless, an
improved pluralism can generally be depended on to yield more just results
than a decision-making process where poor people's and minority groups
are effectively denied a seat at the bargaining table. Yes, as Bellah cautions,
newly empowered groups are indeed capably of inflicting injury on others.
But in a great many more cases, improved pluralism—the empowerment of
previously powerless groups—will help lead to substantive fairness, a more
equitable distribution of results.

As I earlier confessed, I initially saw Bellah's analysis and prescription
as quite naïve. In my view, Bellah was a sociology of religion professor who
seemed to have little understanding of the harsh realities of power politics
in American cities. I much preferred the conflict strategies of noted community organizer Saul Alinsky. I even came to believe that the threat of violence and civil disorder—in Bellah's eyes a clear violation of the respect for
each individual's dignity in a shared community—could at times be effective
in advancing the claims of the poor. As Frances Fox Piven and Richard

Cloward observed in *Regulating the Poor,* a quiescent poor get nothing; a volatile poor get something.

Over time, however, I have come to give weight to those change strategies that respect, not corrode, each individual's human dignity. I have also gained a greater appreciation for what can be accomplished by building on what people have in common as opposed to the Alinsky-style strategy of rubbing tensions raw. Even where the Alinsky strategy proves effective, there is something ugly in a politics of rawness that dehumanizes the target of a political action and drains the humanity of the group members who are so willing to deny the dignity of others.

Today, even Alinsky-style organizations have moved away from protest and have given a greater emphasis to service provision as they have assumed responsibilities for running low-income housing, day-care centers, and other programs that make a real difference in people's lives. Service provision is realistic radicalism; rather than emphasize confrontation, community organizations today have turned to partnerships with outside actors in order to find the resources to make real, substantive improvements in people's lives. There is no need to resort to the raw politics of conflict when viable alternative strategies can be identified.

Robert Bellah and his colleagues have pointed to the importance of reviving America's second language of community, obligation, and social justice. Despite my continuing disagreement with Bellah's evaluations of Black Power and affirmative action, over the years I have come to develop a new appreciation for Bellah's stress on community building, moral development, and the respect to be accorded each individual's human dignity. Bellah has laudably attempted to find a strategy for justice-oriented, social change that avoids some of the more disintegrative effects of conflict and violence.

Sad to say, however, sometimes power and intimidation—not reason, dialogue, and mutual understanding—can be the keys to progressive change. Still, our inclination should normally be against such action; such strategies should be used rarely and with great reluctance. Consensual strategies that appeal to more universal values (including the values enshrined in the American democratic and biblical traditions) often provide viable routes for social change. As the civil rights movement in the United States and the 1989 Velvet Revolution in Eastern and Central Europe have both clearly demonstrated, much can be accomplished by conceptualizing a moral politics based on a shared humanity—including people's shared religious traditions and yearnings—as opposed to a politics conceptualized only as the competitive, pluralistic interplay of conflicting group interests.

Over the years, I have been engaged in an intellectual struggle with Robert Bellah. But the struggle has been most unfair, for Martin Luther King, Jr. and Vaclav Havel have proven to be extremely powerful allies of Bellah in pointing to the potential power of change strategies based on communal values and a positive moral vision. Havel, as a result of his disappointments in office, may have in recent years moved closer to my own more realistic and less moralistic conceptualizations of politics. But on the whole, it is Havel, King, and Bellah who have largely won the intellectual struggle—nay, the moral dialogue—in which we have been engaged.

Stories and Reflections on Learning to Care

Margot Kennard

When I arrived to direct the academic service-learning program at Olivet College, a small, private liberal arts college in Michigan, I saw this position as a perfect way to merge my academic interests with my experiences as a community activist. Like many of my colleagues who came of age in the 1960s, I looked at service-learning through lenses shaped by my past experiences—working in and with the community to create a day care center, a women's health clinic, or an after-school youth program. Seeing the college's service-learning program from the perspective of the community matters to me.

A couple of years ago at a national service-learning conference I heard McClellan ("Mack") Hall tell a revealing story. Mack is the director of the

National Indian Youth Leadership Project and coordinates the Turtle Island Service-Learning project for Native American youth. When he told the elders on his advisory council about the Turtle Island community service project, they responded: "Community service—we don't have a word for that in our language. I suppose they have a need for it." Of course the "they" refers to non-Native white people. I like this story because it eloquently illustrates that when people are naturally cared for within their culture there is no need for a project to teach them how to care. Mack's story also points out that our concept of service exists because something fundamental is missing from our society. How does a society like ours, at the start of the 21st century, re-integrate an ethic of caring into the culture?

As I work to develop our service-learning program at Olivet College, I find I am constantly challenged by the question of how to move students beyond a superficial self-serving notion of service to a view of service that values a collaborative, partner relationship with the communities we work with. When students talk to me about how good it makes them feel to help someone who is less fortunate, my skin gets prickly and I struggle to hold back signs of my disappointment. After a great deal of contemplation on this situation, I have come to believe that students move beyond paternalistic service when they develop a sense of care and connection to those community members they are serving. So, what does it means to care, and how do we learn to care?

I've gone about addressing this profound question through a variety of methods: reviewing pertinent literature, conversing with colleagues in the service-learning field, as well as family and friends, and reflecting on my life story and how I learned to care. Before I share these stories I need to define what I mean by care and an ethic of care.

The question of what it means to care has been widely explored by feminist scholars, beginning in the 1980s, in fields of psychology (moral development) and philosophy (ethics and moral theory). Because it is outside the scope of this essay to review that literature, I look to the work of Nel Nodding to provide a definition of what it means to care. Nodding puts it simply: "Caring is stepping outside of one's own personal reference and into the other's. I receive the other into myself, I see and feel with the other."

By defining care as a feeling with another, rather than the idea of putting oneself in the other's shoes, Nodding makes a distinction between a rational process of understanding and the emotional act of making connections to another, of becoming connected to another by receiving them into one's self. To see oneself in relation to others and to establish and maintain a sense of connection are key elements in a feminist definition of what an ethic of care means.

As I have explored this topic, I have located a few important sites where learning to care develops. For most people, the first phase of learning to care takes place within the family. I learned what it means to care by being cared for by my parents, Marion and Albert. They were kind, physically affectionate, and interested in all aspects of my life. If there was anything that set them apart from other loving parents it might have been that both of them were very empathic. They were so tuned into me that they could immediately read my feelings, whether I felt happy or sad. I once saw a saying on a billboard that captures how emotionally connected my parents were to me: "Empathy is your pain in my heart." I felt lucky to have a father who showed his emotions, something that was not that common for a male parenting in the 1940s and 1950s. No matter how busy my father was, he always made time for me, and he listened to me when I needed someone to talk to.

Learning to care outside my family was in many ways shaped by the community I was raised in—Madison, Wisconsin. Madison, the capitol and the home of the University of Wisconsin, also has a long history in progressive liberal politics. During the 1950 and 1960s there was much public debate concerning social issues such as civil rights, poverty, and the Vietnam war. It was easy for that liberal discourse to filter through to those institutions that greatly impacted on me like my church, my schools, and my family. Even though these social issues did not directly affect me, listening to adults talk about these problems provided a context for my developing sense of caring for others.

When my parents first went to Madison in 1944 from a small town in Pennsylvania, they did not have much money. They moved into an apartment in an older section of the city, close to downtown. It was actually a wonderful neighborhood with much diversity, especially in terms of economic class. The center of the neighborhood was the elementary school, named after Father Marquette. One of the best things about our neighborhood was how easy it was to take the bus up town to the center of the city and the UW campus. Fortunately, my parents allowed me considerable freedom travel to those areas.

My parents, especially my father, were politically conservative and neither of them openly advocated for any liberal causes. However, they were unusually tolerant of diverse opinions and my younger sister and I felt free to articulate more liberal views, many that my parents did not agree with at all. My dad was quite philosophical; he loved ideas and was very articulate both in writing and speaking. For example, he often quoted people he respected, like Ralph Waldo Emerson and Eric Hoffer, the longshoreman-turned-philosopher. Dinner conversations were lively and even if there was not much agreement, he showed respect for me by encouraging me to form my own opinions.

During high school I was out of the house at least three nights a week. I belonged to a variety of organizations, such as the Madison Youth Council, Mariner Girl Scouts, and church choir. Many meetings were held downtown and attracted teen-agers from all parts of the city. The liberal climate of Madison also influenced my school experience, especially high school. My teachers were often graduates of the UW and themselves influenced by the radical progressive environment there in the 1950s. For example, I remember my high school history teacher talking to our class about the positive aspects of liberal social theories like socialism and communism. While my high school was not ethnically diverse, the students came from families who represented a wide spectrum in terms of economic class, from blue collar workers employed at Oscar Mayer Meat Packing Factory, to high power corporate executives who lived in mansions overlooking Lake Mendota.

Still, the most difficult part of my transition from learning to care within my family to caring for others outside my family was coming to the realization that my parents did not always look at the world in the same way I did. An event that occurred when I was 13 years old remains today as a crystallized moment, signaling that I was crossing the boundaries that surrounded my family's circle of care.

In 1958, my family took a vacation to the South to visit my aunt and uncle in Georgia. I remember well how disturbed I was at the visible signs of segregation and Jim Crow laws, like the "Whites Only" signs above restrooms, water fountains, and other public places. My discomfort became more personal when we stayed at my relatives' house. My aunt and uncle, who appeared to me to be economically somewhat lower middle class, employed an African American woman to do their household chores, like washing dishes and cleaning the house. What bothered me the most was the way my aunt and uncle treated her as if she was their servant or maid. It was the first time in my life I had experienced this kind of power imbalance, one of race more than economics, in such a personal way.

Equally upsetting to me was talking with kids my age, like my cousins, who told me that they would never go to the same school as African American kids, even though the laws had changed. But I was even more disturbed and hurt when I found out my parents did not share my concerns. Instead of being upset at these signs of racism and white privilege like I was, my parents seemed to excuse it all by saying, " Well, that's how it is here in the South." The parents I knew were caring people who showed me love and respect. How could they care for me and not care for people outside of our family, especially people who were being treated unjustly? But it was also my parents who supported and encouraged my involvement in the community, and it was through this community involvement that I learned to feel connected to people who were not the same as me. Even though my views on politics and economics differed from my parents, the caring they showed me provided me with a foundation upon which I could develop a caring self.

I left home to attend a small liberal arts college, much like the one I teach at now where issues concerning social justice were passionately discussed. It was 1963 and I was completely caught up in the historical moment, particularly the war in Vietnam and the civil rights movement. Most of the students at my college were very much like me. My feelings of empathy with another were fostered through readings, conversations, and the media. It wasn't until I graduated and joined the Peace Corps that I had what Cheryl and Jim Keen, Laurent Parks Daloz and Sharon Daloz Parks, the authors of *Common Fire: Leading a Life of Commitment in a Complex World* written in 1996, call a "constructive engagement with the other."

What distinguishes a simple encounter from a constructive engagement is a feeling of "empathic connection" with the other, a "recognition of a shared capacity for the feelings that lie at the core of our essential humanity: fear, joy, yearning, delight, suffering, hope, and love." During the two years I served in the Peace Corps in Ethiopia, I had many such experiences with empathic connection.

The training for the Peace Corps program took place during the three summer months in 1967 at the University of Utah in Salt Lake City. All 100-plus volunteers in this training program would eventually serve as ESL teachers in elementary and secondary schools across Ethiopia. The Amharic classes and the culture and history classes were all taught by native Ethiopians who were attending universities in the United States. Many of them had worked for the Peace Corps in previous training programs.

Our facilitator was an Ethiopian named Tadessa who was attending the University of Minnesota. He asked the group to share why they had joined the Peace Corps and why they wanted to go to Ethiopia. This was a question I was getting used to answering—my parents asked it, as did many of my colleagues. I thought my answer was honest and truthful. I told him that I felt I was very privileged since I was lucky to be born in the United States. I had received a good education, including a college degree, and I could afford to volunteer for the Peace Corps for two years without a negative impact on my family or my future career. I wanted to go because I felt I should give back by volunteering to help people less fortunate than me.

I was shocked and completely taken off guard when Tadessa challenged my answer in what seemed like a hostile manner. He asked if I was going to help people who were different from me because they lived in a poor third world country and lacked things I had like education, health care, media and so forth. It was one of the most uncomfortable moments of my life. I felt so embarrassed I didn't know how to respond. I felt he was making me look like some rich, politically naïve do-gooder white woman who was going to Ethiopia to save children.

Fortunately for me I was able to work through my embarrassment and anger and listen to Tadessa's message. He was making the point that while Ethiopians were economically poor compared to Americans, they were rich in terms of their ancient history and culture, including art, literature, and philosophy. Although we thought we wanted to give of ourselves, in the end it would be the volunteers who would receive much. That turned out to be so true. Based on my experience, I regard Peace Corps as a model of a service project built on an equal partnership or mutuality. It was apparent from my training that Ethiopians fully participated in the design and implementation of the training. They knew what volunteers needed to know in order to be effective in the country. The message we received during training emphasized the importance of learning the language, along with social norms and customs so the Ethiopian people would accept us.

I worked as a member of the teaching staff at the Marege Hiwot Haile Selassie Elementary and Secondary School in Ambo, Ethiopia. It was a unique experience in community building. I was regarded as one of the staff; I was never viewed as more privileged because I was an American, a native English speaker, or because I was a volunteer. My headmaster, Mr. Yilma Workneh, supported my efforts as a new teacher and helped me feel welcome in the school. I felt that all of the staff, regardless of their race or nationality, shared a common mission: to provide the best education possible for all the students. The school operated as a real community of care.

Coming back to the United States in the fall of 1969 was a difficult time in my life. One of the most painful areas of re-adjustment was job-hunting. Even though I never made a career decision to become a teacher, I felt, after the positive experience teaching ESL in the Peace Corps, I had become a teacher. Fortunately the state I returned home to made that happen. Due to a teacher shortage at that time, California certified those who had teaching experience in the Peace Corps in lieu of a teacher preparation program in college. The only teacher preparation I received was during the three months of training in ESL. In addition to learning ESL methods, I also spent a month practice teaching at a school on the Navajo Indian Reservation in Blanding, Utah.

So, in December, a few months after I returned to the states, I received a California Standard Teaching Credential for elementary teaching, issued for life! By January I was hired by a school in Sacramento to take over a first grade classroom where the regular teacher was leaving in the middle of the year. My preparation for taking over this class was to spend one-week observing the regular teacher before she left. When I look back on that period of my life I am still amazed that at age 24 I had the courage to walk into that school and accept that position. I felt like an imposter. I had to pretend I knew about classroom management and behavior, knew how to teach non-readers to read, knew how to keep 25 six-year-olds busy with meaningful seat work, and the most challenging for me, how to decorate a large bulletin board with a cute theme, usually related to a holiday.

My struggles with my lack of proper credentials and necessary teacher preparation were intensified by the culture of the school. Particularly painful was an absence of support and advice from the other teachers. It was the "closed door" policy—you went into your classroom, alone, shut your door, and taught. In the few places where teachers gathered, such as the staff room, I quickly learned that if you asked questions others saw it as a sign of incompetence, a sign that you lacked the skills to be a good teacher.

In addition to putting on the disguise of a "competent" teacher, I was also hiding my political and spiritual self. I had returned to the United States from my Peace Corps experience in Ethiopia with a new level of political understanding. When I applied this political understanding to every day events occurring around me in 1970, I felt frustrated and angry. I was especially angry that after seven years, the United States was still at war in Southeast Asia. I was also angry about social injustices, especially racial discrimination and poverty that directly affected the students in my class. But I was afraid to share any of that anger with any one I worked with at my school. I was afraid the other teachers, whose views were much more conservative than mine, would find me too "radical" to be a public school teacher. I tried not to openly disagree with their views or say anything that would be regarded as "controversial." I was relieved when the end of the year came and I resigned my position. I left public school teaching to join a growing movement in California in alternative education, often referred to as free schools. I was sad to leave the public school because I felt I was letting my students down. I knew that the families of most, if not all, could never afford the tuition of a private alternative school. But I needed the alternative school environment to reconnect with myself and find some balance between my values and my life work.

Ten years later, as a graduate student in curriculum and instruction at the University of Wisconsin–Madison I tried to connect my growing understanding of educational theory with my experience of becoming a teacher at Elder Creek Elementary School. As I attempted to situate my experience within a theoretical context, I learned that I was actually similar to many first-year teachers, constrained by fear. Particularly high on the list is fear that comes from the principal or another teacher walking by a classroom door and judging the teacher by the amount of noise and chaos coming from the classroom. I also learned I was not alone in the tension I felt trying to create a caring classroom community while remaining in control of the environment and students' behavior. The perceived need to establish an authoritative role with students conflicts with the desire of many teachers to develop caring relationships with their students.

I think my immaturity and my lack of confidence prevented me from seeing that I had another alternative—to stay right where I was in the public school and learn to teach against the grain, joining teachers who are agents of change and who struggle to reform education from the within the classroom. These are teachers who are often at odds with the administration and other teachers and not always seen as good teachers. I have respect for these teachers and I feel I have much to learn from them. I believe that if schools are to become communities of caring where children learn how to care, it is necessary to learn from these teachers.

In my current position at Olivet College, I serve as the Director of Service-learning, but I am also a half-time faculty in the education department where I teach courses in both the undergraduate teacher education program and in the graduate masters of arts in teaching program. From this position I hear many stories about expectations placed on teachers today to take over many of the traditional parental responsibilities, including teaching morals and ethics. There is pressure on schools to expand their mission into caring communities where teachers can help children cope with the pressures of divorce, single-parent families, poverty, gangs, and violence.

Unfortunately, teachers' stories reveal that schools may be ill suited to fulfill this mission. A research team from the University of Indiana spent the year 1995 in two middle schools exploring the topic of what it means to care in schools. Their findings of missed opportunities to demonstrate care are disturbing but, based on my past classroom experience, completely understandable. Researchers found that the structure of the school day left little space or time for interpersonal interaction, and that during class time teachers were clearly in charge, using traditional learning strategies in which caring interactions were not encouraged. Time in class was spent on activities that would improve test scores on statewide-standardized tests. Themes of caring were rarely discussed even if course content could have generated such discussion, such as a lesson on the Holocaust. Outside of the classroom, time constraints and structure offered few opportunities for students to practice caring or be recognized or rewarded for it. The research team concluded that in such a climate, where schools are rewarded for individual achievement, creating caring communities are unlikely.

However, I believe there are teachers who go against this grain, and they can inspire all of us to see it is possible to learn to care in school. I met such a teacher, Karen Rose, when she was a student in a course I teach called "Building Learning Communities," which is a part of our masters program. In the class I encourage students to contribute their experience in creating communities in their classroom. During her presentation, Karen described in great detail the curriculum she has developed to create a caring community in her fifth grade classroom. I remember listening to her and thinking that what she was sharing was not about techniques or lessons, but learning from the heart. At the end of class I asked Karen if I could observe her. She graciously agreed.

Karen teaches in a small town of 5,000 located ten miles from a major metropolitan city in Michigan. She describes the residents as mostly blue-collar workers who commute to jobs in the nearby city but don't want to live in an urban environment. They also do not want their kids going to urban schools. Karen's intermediate school (grades 5–6) is predominately white, as is the town. Her curriculum for building community in her classroom is drawn from *Tribes: A New Way of Learning and Being Together*

(1995) by Jeanne Gibbs and from her work as a youth minister in her local Catholic Church. She also took a college course that provided in-depth training on the Tribes curriculum.

In her book *The Challenge to Care in Schools,* written in 1992, Nel Nodding states that teachers have a responsibility not only to create caring relationships but also to help their students develop the capacity to care. While Nodding's work is valuable for creating a vision of what could be and should be, her language often seems academic and abstract. As she herself states, "The picture painted here is so vastly different from the one pressed on teachers currently that it seems almost alien." Nodding's vision of a caring classroom includes four components: modeling, dialogue, practice, and confirmation. She defines these components in the following way: Teachers model caring when they treat students with respect and consideration and encourage students to treat others in a similar fashion. Teachers show students how to care by creating caring relations with them. Teachers engage with students in genuine dialogue when it is open-ended with the outcome or decision undetermined at the beginning. The importance of finding time and space for students to engage in dialogue honors their voice. Teachers develop an ethic of care in students by giving them opportunities to practice and experience caring. Finally, teachers confirm students by affirming and encouraging a vision of a better self. When I looked over my notes on Karen gathered from classroom observations and interview transcripts, I found these four components clearly illustrated.

The components of modeling and dialogue were well illustrated in an interview I conducted with four students who were in Karen's classroom a year ago. I asked them to give examples of ways in which her class was different from their other classes. I expected their responses would address the activities they participated in daily as part of Karen's community building curriculum. Instead, they gave examples of things Karen did to show respect for them: "She let us have a bottle of water on our desks, so when we were thirsty we could get a drink. This year we can't even get a drink after gym. . . . She told us we could only eat healthy food for snacks, no junk food. . . . During reading we could sit anywhere, not only at our desks, and if we were talking to each other during class, she would say, 'Shhhh, you aren't supposed to be talking right now.' We'd say OK and stop. This year we get sent out in the hall."

In Karen's classroom, opportunities for dialogue take on a variety of formats. During one visit to Karen's class I observed an example of dialogue when a student shared information about himself with his classmates. Josh began this sharing session by showing the class a poster which included pictures of himself with his grandfather, his cat and dog, and vacation pictures taken when his family visited Washington, D.C. After Josh shared personal information about his family and things like his favorite food, Karen invited classmates to also ask Josh questions about himself. These questions included "What do you do for fun with your free time," and "What is your favorite sport, music band, book, movie, subject in school?" Having a student of the week is more commonly found in an elementary classroom than at the middle school level. By including it in the school day, Karen shows her students that it is important for them to know about each other, including information about families, pets, and hobbies.

Another example of the value Karen puts on creating genuine dialogue comes from my interview with her. Sometimes Karen struggles with how to balance her authority as a teacher and her desire to involve students in decision making concerning how the class will function. As she put it, "Sometimes it would be easier to put my foot down and say 'do what I tell you to do.'" When I ask her what she does instead, she explains that when there are problems affecting the whole class they will have a class meeting. "I have them talk about what is happening in the classroom. I ask them what are the things that aren't happening right now? What's missing? What are the reasons for it? My approach is what do you want for this classroom and for yourself? So then we come up for a plan to solve the problem."

Karen is concerned that dialogue in her class is genuinely open-ended and students do not think that decisions are predetermined. She says, "I don't want any students to come back to me and say I am a phony," meaning she doesn't want students to think that when she holds a class meeting and asks for their opinions and suggestions she already knows what action she will take because she holds authority over them. Because Karen spends the last half-hour of every day doing some kind of community building activity, her students have a wide variety of opportunities to practice caring interactions.

When I began working with Karen there were two questions I wanted to explore. The first one was a very practical one. What did Karen do to create a caring community in her classroom? But my second question was more abstract and less concrete. How did Karen develop into a person who would want to teach from an ethic of care perspective? In order to reveal this I asked Karen to talk about her childhood and her family in terms of role models and other things that might have influenced how she learned to care and become compassionate. Immediately Karen's face lit up, and she talked about how she learned about caring from her mother who was a role model for her.

"My mother is someone who is always doing something for someone, for her service is a way of life." Karen explained when she was growing up her mother did things like volunteer regularly for Meals on Wheels. She even took Karen along with her as she delivered meals to the elderly, an activity Karen valued primarily because it meant "spending time with mom." As Karen talked about her mother it was clear to me that she learned to care as a natural part of growing up in a family where she was loved and treated with kindness. To illustrate this, Karen described her mother as someone who had a way of making Karen and her sisters feel special. "She just has this way of doing things for each daughter—like taking us out one at a time to go shopping or to lunch—so she could have that time alone with each of us."

In addition to her mother, Karen also named her participation in community service during high school as another influence that nurtured her understanding of care. Like her mother, Karen volunteered for Meals on Wheels. "It sounds awful, to give up your Saturdays to drive around giving food to these old people whose houses smell. But when you do it and you meet these people and see their faces . . . you have these interactions where you feel your heart swell. I got very connected to these people and I learned a lot from them," Karen said.

Karen's mother also helped her make the transition from caring within a family context, to beginning to connect with people who were different from her. During the interview, as I listened to Karen talk about her experience of learning to care about people outside of her family, I started comparing my experience with her family experience. While our development of compassion may have been different, Karen and I agreed, based on our own childhood experiences, that feeling loved is important in the development of an ethic of care. This led us to thinking about children who have not grown up in an environment where they've felt cared for by someone. Karen says that in her classroom she can see the difference between those students who can empathize and those who cannot. To illustrate this point she describes how the students respond to a story she reads called *Randall's Wall* (1996) by Carol Fenner.

The book is about a little boy whose family is so poor they don't have water. Because he never takes a bath, kids avoid him. So he protects himself by building a wall around himself. According to Karen, students in the class respond differently to the character of Randall. Some feel compassion for him and identify with him as a person, while other students think he should just take a bath. The value of telling this story is that it enables students to get in touch with their feelings and also to hear how other classmates are responding to the characters in the story. When I asked Karen why she thought some of her students can empathize with the character of Randall and others could not, she said, "I think a lot of the kids in my class feel so bad for their own lives that why should they feel sorry for anybody else. When you are fighting for your own survival . . . it's like they don't have the energy to reach outside themselves and feel sorry for anyone else."

At the beginning of this essay I posed the question, what does it mean to care, and how do we learn to care? I find Karen's compassion for students who are "fighting for their own survival" a wonderful illustration of what it means to care in that deep sense Nodding refers to as an ethic of care. Karen receives her students into herself, not as a rational act of trying to understand a difficult home life, but as an emotional act of connecting with another person.

Nodding also provides a framework for addressing the question "how do we learn to care" by elaborating an ethic of care in terms of four components: modeling, dialogue, practice, and confirmation. In this essay I used these four components to demonstrate the way Karen created a caring community in her classroom.

During the year I spent working with Karen and studying her classroom techniques, I learned that we share many common experiences that resonate with Nodding's four components of an ethic of care. For example, both Karen and I grew up in families where we felt loved and cared for. Our parents modeled for us what it means to care for another person by showing us respect and consideration. Our families also valued open-ended dialogue. Our parents encouraged us to ask "why," and listened to us, even when they did not agree with our ideas and opinions. But the place where Karen and I connect most strongly is in the component of practice. Even though our community service experiences were very different—Karen participated in Meals On Wheels and I participated in the Peace Corps—those experiences provided us meaningful opportunities to practice an ethic of care. We especially valued our service experiences because we developed relationships with people who were different from our families.

The fourth component in Nodding's framework is confirmation or the act of affirming and encouraging the best in another person. In the introduction of this essay I wrote about feeling disappointed with students who view their service experiences as "doing good for those less fortunate." I have not always found it easy to affirm these students and encourage the best in them. The opportunity to observe Karen affirm and encourage her students helped me learn that developing an ethic of care requires nurturing. As a result, I have come to value even more the importance time plays in building relationships of mutual respect.

Professions of Faith

Roseanne Hoefel

To Clarence Philip and Anna Margaret Foti Hoefel,
who taught me the epistemology of the heart.
You are here: hold me.

WAKE-UP CALL

Staying awake is a full-time job. After teaching for fourteen years, I have been blessed with the respite a sabbatical affords. This crucial seventh-inning stretch from Alma College has allowed me to recover myself in every sense of the word and in relation to my profession. The perhaps inevitable burn-out which accompanies steady and dedicated teaching, scholarship and service has literally and figuratively brought me to my knees as I've struggled and prayed to find a way to stay in this demanding profession, restoratively and healthfully. This collapse, real or imagined, took me back to my childhood when, after dinner and before homework each night, my father and mother led my four siblings and me in praying the rosary, kneeling on hardwood floors. Devout Catholics operating on the belief that the family who prays together stays together, my parents weekly, and often daily, recited with us the Profession of Faith. With the dawning of a feminist and multiculturalist consciousness in adolescence, I was increasingly unable to profess certain verses, pretending to have a cough or memory lapse so as not to hurt my beloveds.

Gradually, with a historically and sociopolitically informed awareness—along with a painful understanding of Catholic guilt's debilitating potential in my father's 15-year bout with depression—I became a recovering Catholic, channeling the priceless ethical and moral principles my parents fostered into my chosen profession. This choice of vocation entailed a serious leap of faith as the first and as yet only one in my working class family to earn a college degree, let alone make academe a way of life. As I invested heart and soul into my lifelong learning and teaching, this calling emerged both from and into my self-determined profession of faith.

As most, if not all, academics come to realize, though, much in academe militates against the spiritual holism one naively and ideally anticipates. My own exhausted spirit calls the question: How can I be part of the solution rather than comply with or, worse, participate in the dysfunction pervading and crippling academia?

The tragedy of not finding an adequate and constructive answer to this question remains too much for me to bear as I cannot again abandon my profession of faith. This recognition made imperative my quest to seek out individuals—Joe Walser, Eugene Pattison, Jesse Perry, George Gazmararian, Verne Bechill, and Dominic Consolo—who have pursued, protected, and honored joy, while withstanding the ideological and political pitfalls of academe. They have located happiness within active lives of ongoing change agency whereby they never deem themselves quite finished, integrating the inner life of the spirit with their professional lives

My method, simply, was to compile oral history narratives from interviews with a cherished resource our culture at large, and academic culture in particular, fails to tap, to our own detriment: intellectual elders. Here I refer to colleagues who are youthful in their energy output but who, having made a habit of lifelong involvement in their communities, qualify in terms of their wisdom as the equivalent of Native American elders. Alma College has already suffered, prematurely and tragically, the loss of three such beloved elders in the past few years alone, which magnified the urgency, in my view, of securing for posterity the pearls these community leaders have to share with us. These include primarily Alma College faculty and administrators. One holds a Master of Divinity degree and still officiates at religious ceremonies. Another, freshly retired, has been a professor of religion and philosophy for three decades. A third is our campus minister, who will be retiring within the next three years. The thought of their departure, frankly, sends me into a panic, as I believe they embody the soul of our institution and have on numerous occasions—through their diplomacy and care—managed to guide, in some cases even heal, us through difficult transitions and "growing pains."

Other colleagues, recently or newly-retired, have also been gold mines and their "partial" absence is already felt, though our cherished professor from business helps to assuage this ache by offering an oversubscribed course each fall. A professor from sociology has been a spiritual guide for many communities besides our own. In addition, I interviewed the literature professor emeritus who served as a prototype for Robin Williams' character in *Dead Poet's Society,* as not only another valuable resource, but a way of going back to my "roots": his portrait was one which inspired me to choose this profession as a vocation, a calling. As I suspected, talking with him retrieved that sense of this "career" as a life-way.

The elders I was fortunate to interview understand what Jane Tompkins advocates in *A Life in School: What the Teacher Learned*: they surrendered the desire to control time and refused to, as Tompkins puts it, "evacuate the present moment." They intuited the importance of "nurturing the attitudes and faculties that make of knowledge something useful and good." They have nourished hearts both in the classroom and out and have guided their charges toward integration as an antidote to years of institutionally manufactured and sanctioned divided consciousness. Their own practices of serene reflection, introspection, and contemplative awareness have both directly and indirectly introduced students to their own doubts, anxieties, struggles, hearts and capabilities, thereby fostering education as preparation for life. Their stories have helped me address the question Parker Palmer, in *The Courage To Teach,* locates "closer to the bone: 'Who is the self that teaches?'" in part by making "common cause" with these colleagues. With them, Palmer has taught me the ancient meaning of heart as the locus where intellect, emotion, spirit, and will intersect.

As Cheryl and Jim Keen, Laurent Parks Daloz and Sharon Daloz Parks suggest in *Common Fire: Leading Lives of Commitment in a Complex World,* a cross-cultural conception of faith means "something much closer to trust" than belief, dogma, or creed. Sanskrit, they offer, locates the word for faith in "sraddha," a combination of "to set" and "heart": "faith is an activity of setting the heart." Each elder I interviewed has set his heart to variant professional pursuits, cultivating trust in a context of responding imaginatively to and imagining responsively what one of the interviewees for Common Fire deemed "a holy urgency." More subjectively, they are the ones who effortlessly won my admiration and reverence,

becoming kindred spirits whom I felt could help me re-member myself, my
own commitments and promises. *Common Fire*—a book of profound
impact I was fortunate enough to discover after I'd conducted my six interviews—anticipates variations in my own methodology and framework.
Their questions—"How do people become committed to the common
good?" and "What sustains them?"—echo my own opening and closing
questions: "What (who) originally inspired you toward a career/vocation in
teaching/ministry?," and "Who would you 'footnote' as central to your
own admirable centeredness?"

These points of departure and return seem a fitting context for introducing each of the elders, proceeding in the chronological order in which I
met with them between January and March of 1998.

I. BEYOND THE SNOOZE BUTTON, OR AUTOMATIC PILOT

TAKING STOCK

In what initially was a surprising, but became a fairly typical, reply to the
question of original inspiration, George Gazmararian—professor emeritus of
business—said that he'd never imagined a career in teaching. With a major
that moved from history to political science to international business,
George assumed his livelihood would be in finance, so he pursued an MBA
and had arranged for Ph.D. study at New York University when he received
a call from Alma College about an opening. Accidentally, he ended up loving it and crediting the University of Detroit MBA director, Bernard
Landuyt, with directing him toward this unforeseen life choice.

As to his centering force? "Ruth, no question about it!" is his enthusiastic reply, referring to his wife of 41 years. Cognizant and grateful that she sacrificed her career for his, he also speaks of his gratitude to a son and daughter for their unwavering support. He expresses, too, a deep appreciation for a core group of close friends—most of them Alma colleagues— whose relationships he's nurtured and been nourished by over the years. Notably, he recognizes support staff, with whom he has maintained a cordial and respectful friendship he feels we would be wise to develop across sectors.

GO(O)D WILL BY STEALTH

Not surprisingly to me, given my good fortune in having Eugene Pattison as a deft department chair twice over, Gene's impulse toward teaching began as a youngster helping classmates by appropriately facilitating their learning rather than giving them answers. Gene was inspired both by his teachers and the youthful assistant pastor where he was raised. His dual commitment to theology and education continued in college courses that were exercises in mysticism and philosophy. Particularly fond are Gene's remembrances of French professor Margaret Fulley and English professor Henry Klompp. Gene's junior year was made special by conversations with an enthusiastic missionary, Florence Kirk, for whom the Alma College International Center is named. Henry Klugh, Alma's first psychology professor, arrived in Gene's senior year, solidifying his resolve to major in that discipline (though that degree was not recorded until he'd been on the faculty eleven years). Sagely, Gene discerned that psychology courses would assist in both his clergy and teacher roles (he earned a Master of Divinity from Harvard). As Klugh, one of those who encouraged him toward his calling, predicted, Gene preferred the level of discourse available with students in higher education in spite of his secondary certification.

Central to Gene's sustenance are his brother and sister-in-law to whom he refers as "immensely supportive and wisely so": they were/are never intrusive. Pastors he's worked with recently have capably transformed dilemmas into discoveries of spiritual affirmation. His dearest friends, the Stonebruners, have consistently provided "prickly and puzzled" responses that offer meaningful perspective and prompt his sustaining pursuits, such as the symposium on Ohio writers he coordinates and enjoys.

SPIRITUAL MECHANIC(S)

Reverend Jesse Perry, who has been our campus minister for ten years, cites Minister William H. Mulven as the influence who has modeled the difference between being a preacher and a minister. But because Jesse was mechanically inclined, he never really considered ministry as a vocation. He locates the dawning of awareness in Parks and Recreation Department's Henrietta Johnson's observation that he had "a gift" when working with the children's program. But newly married and an expectant father, Jesse deferred that dream for 20 years, working in the interim for the City of Detroit as a trolley bus repairman from 1956 to 1964, when he was laid off. After working as a land surveyor until 1966, Jesse was recommended as an Inspector, receiving four promotions in ten years, putting in extensive hours and leaving his "JLP" mark at several sites. Transferring to the Health Department as a supervisor in 1972, Jesse graduated from Henry Ford Community College in 1982, retired from the city in 1983, enrolled full-time at the University of Michigan-Dearborn, and earned his degree in 1985. By the time he entered McCormick Seminary, Jesse had been involved in youth ministry since he was 19. Over the years, he'd noticed that youth would leave church after entering college, occasionally returning upon marriage—a trend he studied in a Master's thesis completed after an internship at Alma College.

Who centers him, even while he was commuting from Detroit to Chicago and Alma? "Myrna, first and foremost, my best friend," he says of his wife of 43 years; and his elders, such as William Huston who believed in him and "is still here, though now he's Billy." When Jesse graduated from seminary at the age of 55, he expressed his gratitude to the 19 who attended his graduation by providing dinner and lodging. Though he's buried half of his elders, the others are still there when they go home to Detroit. They are a "gift from God throughout [his] long journey."

FROM SOLE-CATCHING TO SOUL-CATCHING

As the prototype for the innovative and awe-inspiring teacher wonderfully rendered by Robin Williams in *Dead Poets Society*, Dominick Consolo— while not affiliated with Alma College—is an elder I admired from afar after seeing the movie that fueled my own desire to enter this profession. It was serendipitous joy to meet and know him personally when he married one of my closest graduate school friends, Susan Richardson. Dom claims he "attended college accidentally," considering he was the son of a mother with a second-grade education and a diligent, illiterate father born in Calabria to a family which lived in a barn and worked for the Padrone on an estate. Dom grew up during the Depression with his father working several difficult jobs, toiling, for example, in a tannery ten hours a day for one dollar a day, remarkably saving half his salary to send Dom's older brother to medical school. In order to assist with these expenses, Dom hired out as a sole-catcher in a sole-cutting factory where he caught 56,000 soles a day for two years.

A rather indifferent student, given his brother's large shadow, Dom's main love was playing the trumpet, the instrument that would change the course of his life. When *Downbeat* magazine featured his hero, Harry James, on the cover, Dom read the issue with avid interest, finding in the back pages ads for students to work their way through college by playing in the college band. Miami University of Oxford, Ohio, responded favorably to his application. Dom was shocked and frightened, feeling completely unprepared for college. The fact that he couldn't read music, and the band was top-notch, exacerbated Dom's homesickness, as he frequently considered leaving. At his roommate's urging he majored in music after volunteering, following his sophomore year, for the Air Corps where he played for three years in the Union Services band.

As for inspirations, Dom cites Thomas Wolfe's *Look Homeward, Angel,* which enraptured him though he had to ration out pages because money for books was scarce. He eventually "gave in," however, and memorized parts of it, pursued a literature major, and began writing poetry. One of his teachers suggested he stay on for a Master's degree and arranged a teaching fellowship. Teaching freshman English, Dom sent as much money home as he'd earned in the factory. He refers to eight professors at Miami and Iowa who exemplified the quality, perception, and sensitivity toward which he aspired. "Many were what they taught, and possessed profound integrity," he reminisces. Dom's mentors sound like my own in that they subscribe to Laurent Daloz's definition of "good teaching," which "lies in a willingness to attend and care for what happens in our students, ourselves, and the space between us. . . . It is a stance of receptivity, of attunement, of listening."

SURFING THE INNER NET

Like many young adults, Joe Walser didn't know what he wanted to do. With a degree in economics, he assumed he'd continue to Law School. After he was admitted to Duke, he heard of Berman Lloyd, a Biblical historian at UNC-Chapel Hill, from friends who had taken his classes. During his senior year, Joe studied with him and fell in love with the literature, the archeology, "all of it," and so continued taking electives. One day Professor Berman prodded him about what he'd really like to do. Joe's reply: "What you do," as Dr. Berman had intuited. He offered to hire him as a research assistant, an impulse which Joe's parents—who had been struggling with him as he agonized over what path to follow—encouraged. Joe then taught at the University of Chicago, Duke, and then Alma College, where he's been for 35 years.

Among Joe's professional ruminations: he's "never been bored a day in his life" and he tries to tap students who seem predisposed to this life choice, continuing the good turn Dr. Berman gave him. Joe would "definitely recommend" teaching, as he finds it very exciting. Ultimately, he urges others to follow their deepest inner satisfaction: whatever offers wholeness and completeness, a quality of "deep-seeded joy." He urges advisees to "go for that!" Poetic and wise, he explains: "your love line will cross someone else's need line." The Keens and Dalozes cite Frederick Buechner's reflection on "vocation," which resonates here: "The place God calls you to is the place where your deep gladness and the world's deep hunger meet." We would do well, he implies, to pursue that trajectory: what we love most. Among those blessings he loves most and credits with his own impressive centeredness are, quite naturally, Kathy, his wife of 38 years, and his children. With profound appreciation, Joe shares that he was born into, raised by, and grew up in a context of rootedness and nurture,

never smothered, but instead supported. He (like I) possessed a great fortune in his wonderful parents; they are part of who he is, what he does and
wants to share. I find myself weeping—the link is deep and current. Joe
footnotes as well his extended family, which branches out to include colleagues, a designation for which we are all most grateful.

MAKING PEACE

Originally planning to be a Methodist minister, Verne Bechill received a full
scholarship ($400 then!) to Albion College. But the politics in church made
him unhappy, so he transferred to Ohio Wesleyan, which he later learned
was his parents' first choice, though they hadn't wanted to sway him.
Verne's mother had attended business college, and his father had an elementary education. With only one faculty member in philosophy and two in
sociology at Albion, Verne found that program too thin; moreover, his girlfriend (and now wife of 45 years) was at Wesleyan, as was Robert O'Brien,
a professor who influenced him toward teaching. Remarkably, six of the 15
sociology majors in Verne's graduating class went on to secure Ph.D.'s in the
discipline, thanks to O'Brien's exemplary manner as a quiet, humble Quaker
who earned their unwavering respect as a person and as a classroom man-
ager. Verne also attributes to O'Brien a Ghandian approach he adopted
when he resigned as clerk of the Great Lakes Regional American Friends
Committee when he discovered that two persons of color were denied serving on the national board.

Interestingly, Verne also notes negative models. Because much of
Shirley's family lived in her birthplace of Atlanta, Verne pursued graduate
work at Emory University where his advisors epitomized exactly what he
didn't want to be. He completed his Masters in nine months and proceeded

to Vanderbilt for his doctorate, where a Ford Fellowship for those pursuing college teaching adequately supported his family of three with another child on the way. He credits their excellent seminars on the nature of teaching as instrumental to his own pedagogy and formation as an educator.

"Definitely Shirley!" is the anticipated response from Verne regarding his centerpiece, though what followed was less predictable. He candidly discussed his son Greg, adopted at five-and-a-half months and diagnosed as lactose-intolerant at nine months. They thought they'd receive a biracial child, as they'd requested a "hard-to-place" infant. Greg exceeded their expectations in this regard, and a pediatric neurologist helped begin renewal and revival after his outbursts of violence, vulgar language, and other difficulties. For 15 years, though they had two biological offspring and another adopted child, Greg consumed all their energies, testing Verne's limits and challenging what he knew about himself. Extremely intelligent, well-read, vocal, and articulate, Greg has now completed medical school and remains the one who's taught Verne—often painfully—more than any of his other children.

A MORNING REFLECTION

I am struck by the generosity and specifity of the reflective conversations I had with these elders. In a sense, their responses to the framing questions are akin to those Cheryl and Jim Keen elicited in the examining of self, agency, and contribution: "What is my work?" and "Who will be my partners?" My interviewees would be among the 75 percent for whom the challenge, support and inspiration of mentorship played an integral role. Their beacons fostered what the Keens called their charges' "energizing competence" and opened the range of possibility and purpose. Both subtly and directly, these influences showed my interviewees that when schools isolate "'fact' from 'spirit' and both from the emotional aspects of life and learning processes," as John Sanchez and his colleagues claim in their 1998 essay "E Pluribus Unum: American Education and Native American Values," they impede cohesive knowing and community. They grew to understand that "authentic learning cannot take place until the spiritual, physical, emotional, and mental elements of each individual are properly aligned." As American Indian elders teach, if spirituality underpins all life, "education that ignores the spiritual," Sanchez continues, "becomes an oxymoron." Each possessed and appreciated a wide array of what the Keen's and Daloz's call "threshold people" and "hospitable spaces." Each of these mentors proffers "the hospitality of a teacher," as Parker Palmer says in *The Courage To Teach,* "who has a fruitful friendship with the subject and who wants students to benefit from that friendship as well." Importantly, in my view, each also tried to be and provide these entities for others by honoring guiding principles, allowing their inner life to inform and shape their professional one, balancing these key facets, and cultivating holistic healthfulness within academe.

II. GUIDING LIGHTS AND BALANCING BEAMS

THE MOST VALUABLE STOCK

Guiding George Gazmararian's career has been his consistent effort to give his best to his students, assuring that they are well-prepared and well-versed in the dynamic field of business, so that they will not become obsolete. By whetting their appetites with *New York Times* news of current events, he tried to excite them beyond the foundation in the classroom. He notes the challenge in motivating students as their priorities shift from learning to socializing. He also acknowledges the "unbelievable" demands of small liberal arts colleges: placements, advising, counseling, committees, and professional development, in addition to enthusiastic and innovative pedagogy. He humbly recognizes the toll such a post took on his understanding and sacrificing family.

In addition to a "To each his own" philosophy, George cites three primary caveats: caring, listening, and compassion. George recommends that colleges assess their expectations with an eye to minimizing the undue pressures that usurp faculty time and energy away from caring. He is concerned, too, that we've lost sight of the critical factor of listening (particularly to what our elders have to teach us) in our self-absorbed, excessive need to hear ourselves talk. Mournfully, he refers to the companion erosion of compassion, especially over the past decade, a loss informing his decision to retire early and akin to other changes, such as students' declining hunger for education. In relation to this dilemma is the quandary of financial aid: while income demographics necessitate some assistance, George ponders whether work-study and volunteerism wouldn't more likely revive student desire and valuing of higher education than "spoiling" them in a venue that sanctions "not working for the prize."

WHERE THERE'S A WILL . . .

As though in answer to George's call, Gene Pattison beautifully and unwittingly fits the bill of a kinder, gentler faculty member. A key guiding principle? Gene listens to students and respects them as people with other stresses and varied ways of growing besides the classroom. Initially, he hoped to overcome his own timidity by engaging with students in these social growth venues as long-time faculty advisor both for the campus paper and for a fraternity. In these capacities, he witnessed their social development and initiative in planning their own enjoyment.

With the preface that he has perhaps "intellectualized" his inner life—who among us hasn't?—Gene refers to a two-week sensitivity training workshop he conducted in Bethel, Maine. His intrigue with the dynamic compelled him to experiment with integrating similar techniques of feedback and mirroring what the students say and feel in his collaborative groups. Overcoming intermittent student frustration when this approach deviated from staying "on-task," the entire class eventually realized they were reflecting Plato's *Dialogues*.

Other strategies enabling balance and holistic health include "books that bring joy," produced by national teacher-training labs, campus novels, and personal psychology, such as *The Transparent Self,* which still resonates for him. Gene expresses a "eureka" upon finding *Control Freaks* (of which he has three copies), case studies of control as a coping mechanism, with analyses of motives. This book taught him how to establish healthy distance from those who rely on control modes by proffering an Aikido dimension in which one "moves with the opponent." Gene has integrated insights from his readings into his methodology, his interactions with colleagues, and the church services he conducts. Enjoying the "appeal of artistry" in crafting sermons, Gene shares with his students that he spends four-to-six weeks preparing and revising to illustrate the writing process. This vocation proffers solace in refuge "outside of his day job." His quiet morning meditation time, in lieu of a newspaper and other mundane distractions, allows Gene to center, upon rising and before breakfast, aware that contemplation occurs in the silence of one's own heart. Instruments in this self-discipline include Peterson's accompaniment to the Bible (Gene will have contemplated 150 Psalms by year's end), and an Episcopal prayerbook.

This ritual bespeaks Gene's belief that "one mustn't live with the job 168 hours a week," even if it means some tasks are left undone. He finds it more meaningful to completely owe oneself to one task at a time, even if it's a three-mile walk each morning, in the summer adding the same distance on a bike (Gene's exercise regimen) or using his Healthrider to ease aches, increase circulation, and prepare him to "face the day."

ENGINEERING FAITH

Though Jesse Perry's specialized coursework in urban ministry trained him to work with a much different population than Alma College, his faith has always been strong enough to trust that God places him wherever he's most needed. This conviction extended to his ambitious triangular commute between Detroit, Alma, and Chicago, wherein he never endured financial or material distress, even during snowstorms. Jesse deems these faith issues similar to the "fit" he felt at Alma, which dispelled any doubts, and the "fate" that—given the internship choice of a church, hospital, or institution—the job the Detroit Presbytery was grooming him for at a church being decommissioned never materialized. Jesse felt a higher power had simplified his decision, with the Alma site at once "new, exciting, and safe."

Jesse credits a mindset with feeling he was never away from his family for the important events. His seminary portion of the week was a "growing time": prior to then, he'd never been apart from Myrna (his wife of 44 years) for more than two nights (and that when he took youngsters on retreats). When Jesse's children were young during the 60s and 70s, his daughter started the tradition of family meetings to discuss goals and aspirations. To this day, he credits the smoothness of their lives to the collectively determined decisions. Together they managed the pursuit of Jesse's lifelong dream of ministry such that their standard of living wouldn't diminish and no one had to sacrifice upon his retirement from the City. The greatest loss in relocating from Detroit to Alma has been of their African-American community, though sustenance arrives with their frequent visits. Because no one in his family tries to control situations, they've always been able to "adjust to the flow" and avoid unnecessary pressures. This disposition has enabled him to enact a "ministry of presence" on campus, with drop-in availability and his phone number listed everywhere. Jesse's philosophy: ministry is about serving those in need and "preparing them for what awaits."

SOULSTICE CELEBRATION

Like Gene and Jesse who take their cues from the ministry, Dominick Consolo's spontaneity, inspiration, and improvisation in the classroom all sprang from his avocation: musicianship. He loved teaching because it was "promoting a worthwhile product (literature), earning student attention and rewarding them for it," all of which have counterparts in his leading the band. As in Robert Frost's poem, Dom's "object in living is to unite/ avocation and vocation." Dom consistently sought a spark to serve as a catalyst to engage the class in active discovery, his primary goal to reach students and foster a sense of inquiry. He understood early that literature enlarges our humanity, that without it we wouldn't be fully human. Artists write in order to understand and find language for the human condition; students respond, thus, to a literature that essentially reads them. According to Dom, then, literature thereby offsets loneliness and helps us to "create better fictions for ourselves to live by."

Dom's inner life can't help but enter the profession as he's always let his "soul hang out" with the students, sharing himself openly in mutual affection and appreciation (to be sure, the Sicilian way my own mother modeled for me). Literature lends itself to having the spirit be part of the "total teaching self." In fact, to stem the tensions within the academy today, Dom asks us to consider: to what extent does teaching material that deals with the heart, human conflict and potential resolution become a substitute for relationships within the human community? He urges us to ponder whether, or how, classroom humanities can transfer to communal interaction. Policing the inclination toward self-satisfaction and arrogance, Dom believes everyone has to forge her or his own form of action.

While it may be difficult to avoid politics in any profession, the literature itself has aided Dom in sustaining a sense of balance, as has his acceptance of change as constant. His teleological sense of amelioration and the affirmation inherent in teaching made empathy an integral element in his professional monitoring processes. For example, as a department chair assigning courses and committees, he would ask himself: Would I be content with such a schedule? While he wishes he'd have had a stronger sense of organized religion—which he'd replaced with healthy skepticism/agnosticism—Dom ever maintained a "sense of mystery, awe, and wonder in the face of what is"—and, of course, "a good glass of wine."

CASTING A FORTIFIED NET

As is evident to all who have the good fortune of knowing him, Joe Walser does not see ministry and teaching as separate. Though he's careful not to "sermonize" in class, he believes we should "profess" our positions if and when students prompt us. Joe feels deeply connected to a tradition, family values, institutions, a world view. These help him to articulate a life.

"Religio," he explains, etymologically means "to tie things together"—this helps him to construct a livable world, at the center of which are beloveds from whom he learns and with whom he grows. Neither nihilistic or suspicious of authority figures, Joe believes in a "sacred reality at the core of life," a holy being which grounds the foundations we build with students and friends. Grace, he contends, rests in recognizing the gifts that keep him alive and aware, attentive and intentional. For Joe, "God, Christ, the Holy Spirit and their manifestations hold life together."

When Joe surfs the "inner net" of his inner self, prayer or dialogue occurs which is open to the heavens, the world, and the self. He deems prayer, in part, a conversation about what is important: "What am I willing to do? What might be important to others?" These questions, and their answers and implications, inform "the larger cradle of the sacred." The penultimate inquiry, "What is important to God?," exacts that we "be quiet" so the silence can speak. For Joe, this self/God talk occurs frequently, especially when preparing, delivering, or reflecting on a sermon. At home, he and Kathy have meditations at breakfast. Joe muses that when cynics scoff at the idea of prayer because a Higher Power ought to be self-sufficient, he responds: "God doesn't need prayer, I do!"

Morning prayers are an ever present rite of their day, one which brings them to consciousness. In our hectic lives, Joe recommends that we schedule time for reflection and togetherness as a beam for balance. For instance, when his children were preschoolers, he bathed them at 7 or 7:30 P.M., regardless of work demands, and his son and daughter still recall this fondly. In addition, the family would leave town on weekends fairly often. He wanted them to know that "Daddy never lived at school," that there was never a time he "lost sight of priorities." Always, he emphasizes, "family came first." Because church and students are also near the top of his list,

Joe schedules time for these "objects of [his] love and devotion." Yet he acknowledges the need to set boundaries with these entities in our lives.

As the campus chaplain three times, having been ordained in the Dunning Memorial Chapel for ministry on campus, Joe now works with various churches in the Presbytery. These congregations, too, understand and honor his diverse obligations. Overall, Joe is less inclined to agonize (as he used to) about his choices now; he quips: "As one grows older, one realizes he doesn't have to be immortal."

As a postmodern sort of campus chaplain now in the sense that he mediates conflict toward resolution, Joe's role consists of attentive, sympathetic listening which prods colleagues to honor civility in the context of their professionalism. His motto? "You don't have to like someone to work with them; you can disagree and maintain divergent vested interests and still be civil in the larger context of the college's mission." He encourages colleagues in the midst of personnel and other difficulties to commit themselves to "hang in there" and focus on their own role in the conflict. This frequently leads to a shock of recognition in terms of one's accountability or culpability. Joe suggests that in some cases one can end up rather liking whom s/he thought s/he disliked.

Cognizant of the need to provide a space for healing, Joe shares the vision of the college's larger purpose wherein everyone is important and has something valuable to contribute. In such a context, when one member is gone or hurt, the circle of community breaks and all suffer. "More is at stake" than just one person, though, to be sure, even one individual's pain is more than sufficient reason for a proactive, "preventative medicine" stance toward our personal and collective holistic health. "We must give and get, both," adds Joe matter-of-factly. "And we must get out of our egos." Divesting of our egos—a tall, but welcome and essential, order.

PEACING IT TOGETHER

During a four-year teaching post at Wooster, Verne and Shirley Bechill
began facilitating American Friends Service Committee work camps in
1954. After trying about 20 different churches, the first Quaker meeting
they attended "fit" their philosophies regarding equality and absence of
hierarchy. This world view "spoke to [their] spiritual condition" and its
basic tenets have guided Verne's curricular development: Sex and Gender
Roles, Racial and Ethnic Minorities, Peace and Conflict Resolution.
Considering himself a learner, he invites students collaboratively to construct the syllabus, having realized early on that students can't be coerced.
Prioritizing that students learn, Verne has never "bought into" the con-
sumerist tendency to "market" courses (e.g., by appeasing an aversion to
difficulty). He takes pride in their performance, not in whether or how
much they "like" him.

Verne would doubtless agree with Parker Palmer: "to teach is to create
a space in which the community of truth is practiced." Interdependence
between students and teacher lends mutuality and meaning and enables
community to flourish in the welcome absence of self-protective professional
distance, arrogance, and autonomy.

Not distinguishing between his professional and inner life, Verne considers everything spiritual (health, relationships, etc.). Contending that "the
body exists within the soul" (rather than vice versa), Verne respects the
energy field enveloping us. He subscribes to a liberating perspective, one
that is not dualistic. For example, he can't tell the difference between work
and play. "The line is fused to the point where it's just me." He claims further that he just "fell into this fusion" after his departure from Methodism.
Comfortable with who he is, his ego needs aren't such that they have to
dominate. Realizing that teaching brings him the greatest satisfaction, Verne

uses such spaces as the Sex and Gender Roles course to cultivate left and right brain characteristics—the integration of the whole person the main goal—via role plays, role reversals, and structured meditations. While colleagues have dismissed such techniques as "soft," Verne knows these exercises are what stay with the students. Convinced that holistic health is a lifelong ambition (especially after his own cancer surfaced), Verne believes that living a shallow life, selling out, being fraudulent, or bearing steady pain are all worse than dying. Raising children has taught him more than any other endeavor and has contributed to his having a full life—he muses that one can't ask for much more than that except to share it with someone, as has been his genuine fortune for 44 years. He urges the college to know and share itself authentically, fearing that if we aim to be a small university "we will sell our soul."

AN AFTERNOON CONTEMPLATION

As these interviews reveal, spirituality is who we are, and who we are in relation. Perceptive to students' needs and insightful about their inward condition, these elders' teaching has been creative and attuned. They bear powerful witness to the centrality of spirit in our lives and professions. Indeed, it is significant that several did not understand the question I posed: "In what ways has your inner life informed or shaped your professional one?" It occurred to me that the faultiness of the question lies in the phrasing, which assumes a dichotomy to which the wisest among us do not subscribe. Examining the presuppositions in my questions has been instructive regarding my own dualistic biases and evolution of broader vision. Verne mentioned that when students interview him as a spiritual guide, they learn more from how they have to reshape their questions, which raises powerful other questions. We'd all do well to follow Rainer Maria Rilke's timeless advice in *Letters To a Young Poet:* "'Live the questions now . . . then gradually . . . live along some distant day into the answer.'"

Fortunately, the next section of the interviews was not as problematic. These questions cover the elders' most memorable, fulfilling teaching moments, scholarly and professional achievements, personal accomplishments, strategies for sustaining peace and peacefulness as well as fostering these in students, and the integration of social responsibility (e.g., through volunteerism, service-learning, consciousness-raising, or activist awareness and assignment options).

III. WELCOMING THE DANCE OF DAY

LIKE A MILLION DOLLARS
IN THE STOCK MARKET

Understandably, George Gazmararian's students begged him to stay on another year, which made for a tearful departure from "the faces [he] would never see again." The priceless rewards of student success and the pursuit of advanced degrees are "like making a million dollars in the stock market"—and this from a nationally recognized expert in the stock market. George's professional and personal happiness lies in the intangible, in giving rather than receiving—a rare outlook which his parents modeled and instilled. George has willingly shared his knowledge, expertise, and service, offering counsel without the expectation of returns.

Peace has been a bit more difficult to negotiate, given George's penchant as a (self-named) worrier and workaholic. Unlike his children, who share these qualities but also participate in athletic activities to relieve stress,

George never had an outlet to release pressure. Yet he never complained either, because he chose a profession he enjoyed. While he often wonders what course his life would've taken if he pursued the more lucrative New York University path, he's certain that he wouldn't have been as happy. Meeting, helping, and shaping so many young people who later wrote and thanked him for his efforts serves as a continuous reminder he made the best decision.

George feels he was better able to convey these principles to students earlier in his career, lamenting that the current generation is more difficult to reach given the increased egocentrism, aversion to risk-taking and obsessive grade consciousness. He was disheartened the past few years when every time he brought in something extra to enhance class, students would ask, "Is this going to be on the exam?" Also deflating is the trend of under-preparedness or unwillingness to think, evident in their weakness in quantitative analysis and alternative problem solving. In his efforts toward cultural diversity and international understanding, George has cautioned students against blind criticism of difference and emphasized communication skills and global literacy. He strongly urges faculty not to reinforce provincial or isolationist worldviews, and to modify pedagogy in order better to foster complex thinking. He also encourages responsible adaptation to demographic shifts in the discipline: given that now 50 percent of business majors are women, the curriculum needs to better reflect and address their needs.

Ever hopeful, George nonetheless has made a habit of sharing with his students his own community service in the context of their civic obligation to "give back." He thereby tries to shift student sense of reward from the tangible to the intrinsic in order to more effectively diffuse their (perhaps exaggerated?) sense of entitlement and to dis-able the me-ism that society advocates in order to fuel profits. George notes that for five to ten years, business has assumed the impulse of integrating the soul through a process called "organizational development." I can't help puzzling, thus, why the academy is one of the last places to feel and welcome this fusion, particularly since we are in the business of forming a critical, responsible citizenry.

MOMENTS OF GRACE IN AN EASY CHAIR WITH ONE LIGHT BURNING . . .

Gene Pattison's most memorable moments include the epiphany that his classes' interactive strategies duplicated the figures in Plato's Dialogues, and the occasions when students constructively agree to disagree, when his input enriches an *already* engaging discussion. Gene meekly refers to the "surprise of public recognition" as when the graduating senior class awarded him "Outstanding Faculty in the Humanities" title in 1973 and 1981. Also humbly, he alludes to the deep pleasure of placing a prized Annie Dillard article in an important journal with the request to use another piece in an upcoming issue. Though even these *coups* pale near the delight of meeting his most cherished contemporary nature writer who'd been cordially responsive to his correspondence and expressed her gladness that Gene was able to discern something in her work others had not. Also gratifying was the day his critical edition on William Dean Howells, after 12 (!) years of delays, arrived at the Alma College post office.

These joys pervade Gene's quiet times "in an easy chair with one light burning" and lead to serendipity, or what he prefers to call "moments of grace" in the classroom when students honor self-determined parameters and each other during serious conversation. Eventually they volunteer to assume responsibility for peace-making, based on tools Gene's offered for fostering solidarity and reviving student stability. Similarly, Gene tries to enact community service by way of example: tending to campus grounds and gardens, sponsoring the annual writing contest awards, and facilitating social agency through his fraternity's philanthropy goals. Likewise he has openly supported the ethically resistant political trends of the last 35 years, marching, for example, in Lansing in sympathy with Selma supporters. He hopes that such engagements curb students' tendency to insulate themselves from the larger culture and cultures unlike their own.

RETRIEVING KEYS AND RECHARGING BATTERIES

Most gratifying for Jesse Perry are ethnic students' remembrances of him and his contribution to their development. Their calls, letters, and in-person testimonies acknowledge the impact of his generosity, though he feels his capacity to help students who are hurting is impeded when they're reluctant to avail themselves or when they dismiss his input. He hastens to remind them that, at 64, ordained in 1990, he has much insight, advice, and wisdom to offer. Jesse was born and raised to the age of ten in Arkansas—such that, as he haltingly notes, the violence in a movie like *A Time to Kill* or *Amistad* is no news to him. He's witnessed the sweeping changes (and distressing "same old") in the second half of this century with regard to civil rights. He's also participated in the great urban migration North, holding diverse jobs along the way.

These varied experiences he integrates with the "Christ model of personal contact and empathy," evident for example in his wonderful anecdote about helping a stalled driver on Superior Street, one who didn't know (or know what to make of this) African-American Samaritan in her tiny white town. Three hundred or more students have also marveled at his dexterity in getting their forsaken keys out of locked cars. Retrieving elusive keys strikes me as a metaphor for Jesse's search for centeredness: the seeking *itself* has kept him centered. Every year on his birthday, December 5th, Jesse retreats to reflect on his goals and accomplishments. He is committed to this time-out, though it constitutes his most difficult day every year for 41 years. He still actively seeks guidance, particularly given that he and Myrna need to determine what direction their life will take a couple years from now.

Prayer has been both central and centering. In fact, this year launched Jesse's study into prayer: what does it do for us? How do we do it? How (much) does it influence us? Do we actually contemplate the words of prayers? (Here, Jesse playfully confesses that, as prayer leader, he's often thinking: "God, don't let me mess up.") He relates the powerful exercise by students in the campus spiritual development group who spent 45 minutes discussing the Lord's Prayer line-by-line, overwhelmed by its revelations.

Another ritual occurs on a daily basis: morning meditation and exercise, an invigorating and clarifying combination that renews his search and his promises to God (e.g., that he will never preach the same sermon twice, no matter how busy he is and even though his "main congregation has a four-year turn-over"). Jesse also "shepherds a congregation" of 63 members hailing from 12 families in Breckenridge who worship in a 125-year-old building. Because Jesse grew up on a farm with a mother who taught him how to sew, cook, and clean—and who, when bed-ridden, was completely dependent upon Jesse—Jesse is approachable to farmers, seamstresses, caretakers, and homemakers alike. He never presents himself as all-knowing, nor does he tell people what to do. He offers instead a therapy-type, self-determining, compassionate style whereby he relates to them at their level of need, avoiding the pitfalls of condescension, pretension, or presumption.

Because, in Jesse's view, the church is founded on the notion of service, he's been an active instrument in distinguishing service-learning from volunteerism unattached to the academic component. He notes that more students wish to help (e.g., in SOS, Students Offering Services) than there are placements, pre-disposed to this communal impetus as they are by work-camp connections with their home churches. Consistently, though, more women than men are inclined to offer service, and Jesse speculates on the reasons for this disparity. To be sure, females are socialized to serve and find outlets for leadership potential in such venues. He notes that in African-American cultures men are more often receivers than givers, and he speaks of the time he spends divesting young black men of the degrading popularized myth surrounding them as "an endangered species." Even social work organizations have harsher expectations of women and give priority to black men due to their "eminent extinction."

Jesse pauses to consider Alma in relation to matters of race, integral to his own spiritual well-being. While he's been treated fairly well—except by a few clients at the local grocery—his affiliation with the Church and College lends him "sanction," as is the case with local physicians of Indian descent. The common denominator: professions people need. In fact, people often "speak to the color," not the person. When Jesse makes rounds at the hospital, most staff members call him Dr. Lewis, the only African-American doctor on staff. He also notes that Alma—the town as well as the college—has not *needed* to change, as the minute minority population doesn't constitute a threat, let alone a critical mass. Complacent in its comfort zone, the institution needs to reckon with the pragmatics of increasing its ethnic student population. He prays the community will find the keys to greater mutuality and expend respectable energy re-charging all the unique and valuable parts of its body.

THE CHALLENGE OF SYNCOPATING SOULS

One teaching moment in which "nature conspired to help him" occurred when Dom Consolo was teaching Nathaniel Hawthorne's "The Artist of the Beautiful." Cognizant of the themes he wished to discuss, but also that he wanted to leave students with a sense of wonder over whether nature imitates art or art, nature, he found a butterfly on the way to class to beautifully engage the point.

Yet such highs often dovetailed with corresponding lows when Dom wasn't in synch with himself. He'd experience fear and anxiety that as often depleted as energized him. In the former case, he felt acutely the difference between being at his best and teaching "average." If everyone were in a "transcendental fog," he deemed it wiser to dismiss class. As such, family life was *crucial* to his stability. Dom's wife and children were extremely supportive and he enjoyed time with them and his dog. Also significant, his former vocation became a sustaining avocation: he continued to play music throughout his tenure, even participating in a four-language jam session in Israel. These facets of his life brought joy and peace.

As for transferring such elements to students? Dominick's main goal in teaching was to have students grow to appreciate themselves as their own best friends with literature and solace and wisdom offering a sense of peace and resolution. Not surprisingly, many students attested to developing a sense of responsibility to the human community as a result of his classes volunteering, for example, at summer camps with a "transcendental" approach, or joining the Peace Corps. Notably, several moved out of dorms and into homesteads lacking modern amenities but advocating self-sufficiency according to the basic necessities in Kibbutz-like frameworks.

To be sure, this rare group who breaks from conformity contrasts the overall shift Dom notes in student goal orientation: financial independence as consumers who have secured good jobs. This priority is inextricably linked, in Dom's view, to the hyper–grade-consciousness to which others allude. Together they make teaching in the Humanities tricky given its ambiguities and students' attendant frustrations. As advisors for international students, Dom and Susan have painfully witnessed an insidious array of prejudice. Dom urges constant vigilance of one's own, as well as others' tendency toward "oppressive intolerance."

Dom is grateful for the changes he's observed over 38 years, from compulsory chapel attendance and dress code to current trends of a wealthy student body and a modern Jewish female president. The Honors Program (which Dom chaired from 1968 to 1976) has made a substantial change in the student profile, as has the recent prohibiting of residential fraternities (which Dom describes as a "hive of human rights violations," particularly for women, a space "where drunkenness, racism, and anti-intellectualism have thrived for too long"). Dom's hope is that such healthful modifications will better syncopate the oversoul of the student body.

INNERSPACE

Among Joe Walser's heartwarming rewards are student reminders, ten to fifteen years later, of "something delightful" he said. More significant than awards, fantastic lectures, or rare sermons, these "tiny moments" acknowledge Joe has made a difference. Also gratifying are students' "I see" expressions in class, "a joy to witness." If these epiphanies aren't "touched by and rooted in the sacred," Joe muses, "I don't know *what* is!"

Joe's dexterity with etymology is impressive. "Shalom" in Hebrew, he notes, means joy and connection. It has two sides: active and passive. In the latter, it is the cessation of warfare, whereby the Shalom of God extends to one's neighbors. At these times, conflicts with oneself cease such that whole-ness and harmony can prevail. Joe calls this juncture "paradise regained." To define active peace, Joe alludes to Reverend Dr. Martin Luther King, Jr.'s concept of the "presence of justice": *All* must have it for *any*one to truly possess it. Joe is particularly fond of what I would dub peace contagion. He claims that "Other's peace touches ours, and vice-versa. You can't keep it to yourself." And truly, who would want to?

Yet Joe understands that peace can't be coerced. We can, he implies, alert students to the possibility of peace, "nudge them to wake up to it," for example, by pursuing it. Trying to help others come to grips with the great abstractions of life enables them to imagine the probability of peace. Again attending to the power of words, Joe notes that the active pursuit and ten-der sharing of peace make it more a present participle than a noun. It's an ongoing doing and activity. Modeling it—or better, *being* it?—may transfer to students. At times, just opening their eyes to it elicits *their own* response. "Most of us," Joe believes, "really want peace."

One way Joe nurtures this common desire is through his service-learn-ing courses. In one, "Biblical Ethics and Community Service," Joe poses a central question: How did Biblical teachings and communities treat their powerless? Joe anecdotally concretizes such concepts as rooted in the oral tradition of stories dating back to ancient Israel. Focusing on the image of the widow, the orphan, and the stranger within one's gate, Joe shows how it becomes increasingly clear the powerless must be cared for simply because God cares for them. Because most Alma College students have never met a poor person, service-learning helps to flesh out the meanings of such abstractions. Students bring their experiential learning to bear upon their struggle with the concepts and realities of alienation, meaninglessness, and righteousness—which in Hebrew refers to right acts and right relationships.

Joe is heartened by the resurgence in altruism. Students request placements at the Community Café, the Masonic Home for the Elderly, Women's Aid, or multiple venues. In their journals, many note their own background's stark contrast to those who have been neglected or abused. Confronting the exploitation and trauma of women and children lends them a depth of understanding and shifts their sympathy to empathy. These involvements allow students "to taste a real, raw dimension of life," thereby enabling them to see the sacredness in/of their contribution. Joe's own role is as listener or as a "blotter," absorbing all this. Like the interviewees for the Common Fire project, Joe reminds students of the "implicit promise" in community service: "as we heal others, we heal ourselves."

GIVING PEACE A FIGHTING CHANCE

Among Verne Bechill's most rewarding pedagogical experiments was his first systems and macroanalysis class, which was a "tremendous success." In this innovative course, students create their own syllabus around a central subject matter—in this case Central America. Word traveled about this peaceable classroom, for Verne received the following year a phone call from a University of Chicago student inquiring about it. Another memorable occasion was student Ed Kain winning the Barlow Award after Verne had him in six classes, and his selection as one of 11 National Science Foundation recipients in Sociology nationwide.

Ed is among many students whose correspondences attesting to the impact of their coursework with him Verne welcomes. Ed no doubt was among the friends and colleagues who, in the space of three weeks, founded a $10,000 scholarship in Verne's honor upon his retirement. Madeline Hansen, a lifelong activist and playwright, returned to direct and star in *The*

President's Cabinet, a feminist, socio-historical production she dedicated to Verne on this momentous occasion. A rape counselor by the age of 16, as an undergraduate, Madeline found a genuine mentor in Verne, who saw her through to the Michigan NOW presidency upon graduation. In addition to the peace this camaraderie offers, Verne and Shirley often retreat North "to nature." As members of the Association of Couples for Marriage Enrichment (ACME), they also conduct and participate in workshops and retreats throughout the country. He learns more about himself and God in these interactions, which help him have a life apart from the college and maintain balance and a stabilizing sense of humor (all qualities our institution will sorely miss). Always a leader/contributor, Verne—with Shirley and a few other couples—developed the training, certification, and selection standards for ACME facilities, as well as the evaluation forms. They were also instrumental in the linguistic and conceptual shift from "marriage" to "couples" enhancement to accommodate gay and lesbian and unmarried duos.

As his avocation reveals, Verne firmly believes that one cannot teach peace/peacefulness, but must do and live it; modeling, thus, is critical. He concedes that one can teach the tools that give peace a fighting chance.

Because social-mindedness naturally "fits" in his discipline, Verne's main observation regarding service-learning is that it be fluid and smooth, not forced or rigid. He's not terribly hopeful, given the students' decreasing interest in the national scheme and their increasing focus on gainful employment to pay off their debt, and the growing conservatism affecting them within the larger context. He credits his casual rapport and informal atmosphere with minimizing the incivility he's experienced but which other colleagues (such as myself) increasingly bemoan. He has, however, witnessed more ego-centrism and meanness, which he urges us to counter as we continue to strive for peace in the profession.

A N   E V E N I N G   M E D I T A T I O N

As these accounts demonstrate, these elders share philosopher Martin Buber's sense that "All real living is meeting." Throughout their careers, they have committed themselves to encounters which enlarge connectedness and the responsibility that comes with it. Along with the Keens and Dalozes, they recognize "a shared capacity for the feelings that lie at the core of our essential humanity: fear, joy, yearning, delight, suffering, hope, love." These elders's teaching and other endeavors have succeeded in fostering intelligent, constructive, humane responses to the challenges of the ways we live now. They self-nurture this capacity by honoring the need for some explicit form of pause, particularly to recover from injustice experienced or witnessed. They are persons of conviction and integrity.

In various venues, they have modeled for students, colleagues, and others the meeting and internalizing of perspectives and voices unlike one's own—including those who harm us—a practice which liberates and extends the imagination and, hence, the possible. They are adept at recognizing the particular and skillful at discerning it within the whole. This praxis is fueled by their keen and quiet understanding of the primacy of serenity. As such, they are in a unique position to consider, in soft retrospect, what they might have approached differently, if given the chance or the gift of 20/20 hindsight; what advice they'd proffer to less seasoned colleagues, especially for nurturing the spirit while juggling academe's expectations; and what suggestions they can infer from their own extensive dedication to fostering a sense of joy through the long haul.

IV. TWILIGHT RESPITE

INVESTING WISELY

While George Gazmararian harbors "no regrets," he sympathizes with those choosing academe now due to, among other factors, warp-speed technological automation. While faculty must expose students to the new technologies in which they need to be versed, this integration ought not to be at the cost of human interaction and contact. We must persevere, George claims, in our "retrieval and protection of the human element."

George's only remorse rests in his long-time craving for class discussion, which he was not able to promote or prompt much—in part due to the nature of the discipline or to prohibitive class size. Another challenge has been dealing with students who are average, as they require a particular brand of energy and steady motivation, whereas "those with drive, discipline, and ability just need direction." Yet when a weaker student performs well upon graduation, it is especially gratifying.

George enumerates other qualities we would do well to resurrect. First and foremost is trust, the current lack of which is destructive. Obsessed with having everything in writing, we have depersonalized and objectified our relationships such that detrimental tension breeds itself between faculty and administration and between senior faculty and new hires. To counter this trend George recommends patience and the conscientious resistance to fast-lane and by-pass mentality informing the competitiveness and immediate gratification impulses in the culture at-large. Finally, he urges respectful, compassionate, collegial relations wherein faculty faithfully listen to each other, rather than form camps and deter the provost from curricula and education concerns to human resource problems.

With more careful attention to "grace, manners, and propriety,"

George contends, faculty can begin to work as a team again. One practical possibility might be bringing elders and junior faculty to an open conference on such important issues as family needs or the pressures on younger couples. Another is to strengthen and broaden a more effectual mentoring program, perhaps one wherein mentors come together to discuss problems, new faculty do the same, and then they interface jointly and collaboratively in an atmosphere of open-mindedness and mutual encouragement.

THERE'S A WAY . . . AND THEN SOME

Gene Pattison arrived on campus fairly naïve about the realities of being on a faculty. To his surprise, during his first opening Convocation, a condescending senior colleague was dismissive of and rude to him. Much later, when the side-taking into different camps called the English Department dynamic into question, the Provost requested Gene be chair. He was reluctant due to his inexperience in this capacity. Gene didn't share some colleagues' grand delusions, which made them obsess over "getting ahead in their departments and specialties." Rather, Gene was content "to do the best [he] could," describing the invitation in his first year to do a critical edition on William Dean Howells as "nothing more than a happy accident."

CONSTRUCTING AND INSPECTING: A LIFETIME WARRANTY

Jesse Perry replies without hesitation, "No, there's nothing I would change." He's been extremely happy with the path of his life and never *forfeited* his or his family's desires or hopes. Growing up on Aid to Dependent Children,

Jesse heeded his mother who taught him to make the best of any and every situation. For Jesse, this has meant consistently re-tooling himself.

As we construct and inspect our own lives, Jesse recommends we reflect on where we've been and use our experience to gain precision. As we look both forward and back—a metaphor Jesse gleaned from his time in sewers constructing pipelines—we can project our own betterment. Jesse believes that the past grounds and roots us in who we are and, as such, is a gift we have to take with us and, ideally, share with those who need it.

It follows that for Jesse a grounding in one's faith and the capacity to share this freely is essential to joyfulness. Myrna's grandmother is one of his mentor-elders whose adage—"If I can't help you, I won't hurt you"—still enables him to weather with survival humor the vicissitudes of racism. Jesse contends that swapping stories with elders, which includes hearing our own, helps us re-member where we are and have been and also allows us to realize these places and spaces are better than where we could have been: "I was poor and black in Arkansas in the 30s, but I wasn't shackled."

SOUL MATING AND STEPPING IN/TO THE BEAT

Very sensibly, Dom Consolo responds that he couldn't have done anything differently since he hadn't the hindsight at those moments which alternatives would have necessitated. He and other elders seem to inhabit a practical wisdom. He does wish he could have been more savvy in the 70s when the academy began to "indulge in aimlessness." He could have used a more holistic, positive vision. Because he gave his all in the classroom and played in the band every weekend, Dom would like to use these "golden years" to write more, particularly poetry and fiction, which he'd dabbled in throughout his career.

Fortified by attending interviews of candidates for recent teaching positions, Dom senses that educators *choose* to enter academe and stay in teaching because they love it and are successful. Bad or indifferent colleagues can sour this passion, but Dom suggests one "play politics positively" to offset potential spoilage. He encourages us to be pragmatic rather than overly idealistic about what the job demands, its pitfalls, and the tenor of one's home department. Urging us to be "tough-minded and tough-skinned," he recommends the practice of self-assurance, aware of the sacrifices that come with the ivory tower territory. Above all, as his own life illustrates, one should continue to cultivate a sense of self and values, a "hard moral core," and if at all possible, an avocation which speaks (to) one's soul.

NAVIGATING THE WEB OF LIFE

Way cool, as always, when asked what Joe Walser would do differently, if handed the chance on a silver platter: "I'd just do more of everything. I don't dwell on the past." Joe tacitly acknowledges the potentially crippling effect of the "coulda', shoulda', woulda'" trio. Select in his phrasing, as well, with respect to advice for greener colleagues, Joe says: "Just three words: stay in touch—with yourself, all those around you." He assures us: "you'll be okay." He urges us to realize the joy amid the headaches and tears, a golden nugget I take especially to heart given that he follows it with the novel reminder that "sabbaticals make the whole community stronger."

Joe reiterates how essential it is to "stay conscious," and—if necessary *first,* to "wake up!" in the Buddhist sense. He reminds us also to embrace the power in transcending duality so that we can see and touch, taste and smell, hear the whole and imagine oneness.

CHANNELING PEACE

Verne Bechill serenely replies, "No, not at this time. Nothing comes to mind I would change." He's practiced throughout his life what he preaches to us now: "Be yourself. Forget about trying to impress people or meet criteria. Too much energy is wasted on this." And, he would add, on the deluge of mail, about which he implores us to be more selective. Similarly, Verne begs us not to be swallowed up by the endless paper work that accompanies excessive accountability in a system that dishearteningly relies on what's "measurable." On this score, he recommends the seeking and creating of more meaningful and long-term evaluations to reduce what he calls "academic prostitution" of teachers gearing classes toward these devices. To younger faculty, Verne beseeches: "Don't sell your souls or you'll be of no value to yourselves, students, or colleagues." To his fellow older white males: "Embrace *genuine* diversity."

Identifying more as a peace-maker than a sociologist, Verne feels we'd do well not to take ourselves so seriously: "not everything is a barricade issue." He cautions us not to overemphasize where we've been, as this overshadows the vision of where we can go. He wishes other disciplines could follow the lead of those like literature and sociology in not distinguishing between work and play, for herein lies a tacit sustaining of joy. Convinced that "human beings are our most important resources," Verne reminds us that faculty are *not* "replaceable cogs" and should be offered the space necessary to build their own niche.

Given the extensive changes in academe, including the erosion of autonomy and freedom in Verne's view, he's not sure he would recommend teaching, though he wouldn't discourage students if they had a fire for it.

V. CENTERPEACE

These wise men subscribe to the view, as should we all, that the unexamined life is not worth living. When Verne asked that I consider adding to the interview the question "Would you encourage others to enter this profession?," I had to ponder why I had left this reasonable inquiry off the agenda. Did I assume the answer to this would be embedded in other responses, or was I afraid of its implications? Did I fear my most treasured mentors would question my own choice, especially considering my vulnerability on this score, as I had been debating its rightness myself of late? As these mentors anchor my own perceptions of how and who I strive to become, they also challenge simplistic assumptions and impart a more complex kinship with human purpose and accountability. Their charge is the courage to recover, among other jewels, the plank and platform of myself, my own stories, my life, if I truly wish to inhabit a space where everyone possesses the secret of joy, dignity, value, and giftedness. Their illustrative life stories remind me that there's no greater violence than what we do to ourselves and others in the conspiracy to withdraw, though we may invoke this survival strategy intermittently as a sanity measure. If we succumb to this self-protective withdrawal impulse in the long term, though, we diminish our identity and integrity and "lose the heart to teach," as Parker Palmer cautions us. Yet, occasionally and in moderation, we must retreat in order to restore ourselves to wholeness and holiness.

These elders' generous sagacity has opened me to the gravitational pull I felt originally toward the literature I relish and teach. The *discipline* my beloved discipline exacts aids me in discerning between the significant and the inconsequential, as well as recognizing valuable links among them. As Dom and Gene, fellow literature enthusiasts, tenderly reminded me, through this art we gain the clarity to recognize our limitations, the strength to acknowledge them, and the grace to accept and forgive ourselves. Grappling with literature in community better enables us to greet contradiction and welcome paradox for the mystery that resides therein. Among the truths that emerge and evolve from these reflective and critical dialogues are the "radical uniqueness and the fundamental humanity," to borrow Keen and Daloz's terminology, of all literary and real characters. Now, when others ask "What do you teach?," I can reply "people," in every sense.

How are our own stories told in our work? How did I find my story through my elders' stories? How did their narratives become shapings and allegories of my own? The judgment, character, intellect, and vantage-point of my mentor/elders enable me to more fruitfully inhabit these questions with heart and mind open to the answers. Their professions of faith dispel my weariness and magically rekindle my sense of our common journey.

Spirituality in the Service-Learning Design Studio

Virginia North

My primary reason for including a service-learning experience in design studio courses I teach is to increase student awareness of the interconnectedness of individuals, community, and the environment. University design students work in the community to learn about the needs and desires of people in the community. During this experience students may encounter political and social issues that impact their design solutions and affect the connections they attempt to make with the community. This type of experience allows students to become part of the design issue as well as part of the design solution.

David Kolb's model of experiential education influenced by the process of inquiry advanced by John Dewey forms the theoretical basis for service-learning. While there still is not universal agreement for a definition of service-learning, John Saltmarsh describes it, in a 1996 article in the *Michigan Journal of Community Service-learning,* as "a pedagogy of reflective inquiry linking students' involvement in community service with their intellectual and moral development." Saltmarsh states, "community service-learning claims as its inheritance a concept of education that integrates thought and action, reason and emotion, mind and body, leisure and work, education and life, and connects individuals to their community and natural contexts."

One problem with service-learning has been a focus on making students feel good as a result of service that may not be responsive to the needs of the community, but simply meets the requirements of a course or university. To eliminate this problem, I encourage students to think and reflect before and after each encounter during the service-learning part of a design studio course so they might increase their understanding and consideration of the community as well as enhance their inner connections and connections with each other.

Spirituality comes into my service-learning design studios as part of a method to enhance reflection and allow students to relax, slow down, increase awareness, and connect with their inner selves. Contemplative practices such as meditation and reflection are at the core of many spiritual traditions. Use of the term "spirituality" within the design studio is a concern because of the different meanings it can have for people. Spirituality is synonymous with organized religions for some people who then react to the term based on their attitudes or perceptions of these religions. Jon Kabat-Zinn offers a definition of spirituality that is relevant in this case. In *Wherever You Go There You Are,* he says spirituality "means experiencing wholeness and interconnectedness directly, a seeing that individuality and the totality are interwoven, that nothing is separate or extraneous." This definition further emphasizes the need to experience the interconnectedness of person, community, and environment in the service-learning design process.

My interest in exploring the relevance of spirituality in teaching service-learning design studios began during an interactive computer journal experience in a class that met during the fall of 1996. The goal of this journal was to increase connections among students and faculty and between students and a client for which they were performing service. Students could access the conference at home, if they had Internet connections there, or on campus. The conference was structured so students could add topics to the items relevant to the course and project. Topics that began to emerge included discussions about issues relevant to students' performance in the course. Their personal beliefs, including spiritual beliefs, were often mentioned in relation to the balance in their lives that was challenged by demands of school, work, and personal life. These discussions created greater understanding and caring about each other along with a consideration of the more human aspects of the client and community being served by the class.

During this same semester I had reached a point where my own life and career as a teacher had become unbalanced, and I felt disconnected by the conflicting strings tugging at me. I was trying to encourage students to be creative while I had lost my own creative spirit. Parker Palmer, in his book *The Courage to Teach,* discusses the disconnection that teachers sometimes experience when they realize they "thought they were joining a community of scholars but find themselves in distant, competitive, and uncaring relationships with colleagues and students." This seemed like an appropriate description for my disillusionment over the lack of collegiality and absence of respect for ethics I observed within my university teaching job.

The computer conference discussions that addressed the role of the spirit in life, career, and creativity made me begin to realize that I had gradually lost touch with my own inner spirit and was suffering both emotionally and physically as a result. These discussions, however, also showed me that within a community of scholars there were still some who cared about connecting in a positive way with others both to learn and to provide service. The connections students made among themselves and with the client and community encouraged me to develop experiences based on spiritual traditions for future service-learning design courses that allow an opportunity for inner growth as well as external connections to form.

Connecting with oneself is an important first step in developing a creative design process. According to Frederic and Mary Ann Brussat in their book *Spiritual Literacy,* "[e]very culture and wisdom tradition links the arts and spirituality. Creativity is a pathway to the sacred" and "it fuels our spiritual journey." At the beginning of design studio sessions I typically introduce short, focused meditation to allow students to take a mental break from all of the distractions unrelated to the studio that were brought to class. Soft music is played and students are asked to think about nothing specific for five minutes or to focus on their breathing. Some students use this exercise to relieve the stress they brought with them so they can address the issues in class that day. The ability to work creatively is enhanced by clearing the extraneous thoughts and concerns that are distracting to the design issues within the studio, and students are encouraged to use this technique at home before they begin work on their design projects.

While meditation can help at the beginning of a design session, there are still problems that arise with the stress of deadlines and concern about the quality of ideas that can cause blocks in students' creative thinking processes at any stage in a design project. When students begin to show frustration or cease to develop new ideas, I invite them to read *A Creative Companion* by Sark. This book is visually interesting and promises to help the reader "free your creative spirit." Sections can be read in any order, thereby allowing students to easily follow their own paths. So that reading this book would not seem to students like another typical class assignment, I ask students to pass my copy of the book among them and then write on the computer conference about how they feel about their own creativity and what the book suggests to them. This method of presenting the material and students' abilities to read other students' comments on the computer conference generates positive anticipation among those students who have not yet read the book.

Students' expressions on the computer conference indicate that they are connecting with their inner selves as a result of reading *A Creative Companion* and reflecting on it. "Sark showed me," one student writes, "how uptight I am in many different aspects of my life. I just need to let things go sometimes and reading this book helped me be at ease more with myself so I could let some things go." An older student observes: "[The book] made me realize how much of my creativity has been stifled since I was a kid. I think I used to be very creative, making up stories, drawing pictures, thinking of ideas. I tend to think of creativity as not always productive, and so I suppress it." Afterwards, this student began to place more importance on creative thinking during her projects and found that she was able to more easily reach an acceptable solution.

Sark suggests that your spirit is the origin of your creativity. Particularly effective exercises for me involve concentrated observations of nature and sketching and visualizing thoughts and ideas. While an immediate impact on my ability to think creatively is not evident, the freedom I feel with each of these exercises allows me to clarify some of the issues that seem to have blocked my ability to move forward with my own life and work.

While making the inner connection is a first step, the connection with others is an important second step for those who want to work in the design field. While it is common for design students to work together on projects, it is also common for the group structure and dynamics to result in problems. In *Gifts of the Spirit,* published in 1997, Zaleski and Kaufman argue that group behavior is part of spiritual life in many traditional societies where survival depends on group cooperation. This is seen, for example, in Amish communities where harmony in group activity follows their spiritual practices and focuses on meeting a person's spiritual needs. To create a similarly cooperative environment in the design studio, I use two exercises to increase awareness of the interdependent role each person plays in a group activity.

The first is based on the game "Twenty Questions," where a problem must be solved with a limited amount of input. The entire class has to work together to solve a problem and they are only allowed to ask a specific number of questions. This forces everyone to depend on each other to determine the best set of questions, and it also forces everyone to work together to arrive at solutions based on answers to those questions. The level of combined focus on the problem seems to increase the connections among students and the final most difficult problem is solved on the last question. Students write in their journals about how they feel during this exercise. The majority recognize the power of the larger group working together to solve problems and indicate that they would like to work in that type of collaborative environment. The force that is evident in solving the final difficult problem goes beyond the content of each question and individual contribution of each student.

The second exercise is based on a game where students consider an issue while playing a defined role. A single problem-solving strategy is randomly selected by each group, and only that strategy can be used by everyone in the group to solve the problem. This exercise is played at a point in the semester where students have been working in two large groups to develop a design for a community center. Usually, the groups have experienced communication problems and many of the students are upset.

I choose problems for each group to solve that are part of the groups' communication problems. In one group, for example, a student became dictatorial with the rest of the students because she did not seem to respect others' opinions or quality of work. Of course, the group had already experienced this behavior by the dictatorial student and several students had disassociated with the work of the group rather than accept this type of treatment.

The problem the group had to work on was to develop a plan for cooperatively completing the project on time. The strategy they randomly selected was to offer only new ideas and suggestions for solving the problem. Judgmental statements were not allowed nor were negative statements about why something proposed would not work. Each student in the group of seven was to be allowed to respond to the problem without interruption by the others. As the exercise began, I observed that several students provided positive ideas and the others listened. However, when the third student began her recommendations, the dictatorial student had finally had enough and began to judge the student's suggestions. As this began to happen with the fourth student, I intervened and specifically asked the dictatorial student to wait her turn to speak and to then provide only positive suggestions.

In their private journals students wrote about this exercise and how they finally realized that the actions of the dictatorial student had created serious communication problems within the group. Some students reflected on how they felt when the dictatorial student took charge. One student expanded her reflection to other similar experiences and realized that her response to the situation was part of a larger problem for her. This exercise encouraged her to develop alternative strategies for responding to similar situations in the future. Ultimately, the group began to function more productively by improving their connections with each other. Unfortunately, the dictatorial student recorded in her journal that the exercise was a waste of her time. She did not indicate that she realized how her actions contributed to the group's problems.

Another major goal of integrating spirituality in service-learning design studios is to improve student connections with a client and community. One example of a successful connection with a client is a project in the City of Detroit's Empowerment Zone. The project allows students to work with a community group that is developing a manufacturing business incubator that would help businesses that want to locate in the city.

Students are able to meet with people who are developing the business incubator, and this increases their motivation for involvement with the project. The ability to visit the neighborhood and building, as well as a trip through the city, allows students to begin to experience the issues important to the clients.

In one case, unfortunately, students did not show interest in discussing the plight of the city and the role the Empowerment Zone and the business incubator could play in revitalizing an area troubled by social and economic problems for years. Even when I assigned questions relevant to the students' roles in serving this neighborhood, I did not receive a response that acknowledged the social and economic issues the clients face. Students either did not want to discuss how they felt, or did not perceive or understand the situation.

Following a frustrating visit to an inner city neighborhood to meet with a committee of people supporting the project, I reflected on my own commitment to service in a journal entry. "It occurs to me," I wrote, "that I have forgotten just how depressed some areas of the city have become. This project allows the students to connect with a community that is truly in need, however, what about me? I'm not doing as much for the community as in the past. I have lost my connections to the city and the architectural community where I once worked. My current service experiences as a faculty member in a university seem of low value when compared to the needs of the larger community. Spending hour after hour hearing announcements read during committee meetings and trying to write elaborate proposals to make small changes in the university process are frustrating. Furthermore, these required meetings don't seem like 'service' —something I thought I had the freedom to give."

This awareness led to an evaluation of my position as a faculty member in a large university full of bureaucracy. Could I continue to spend a significant amount of my time meeting the needs of this bureaucracy while I ignored the needs of the community?

The following year my design students worked with a client in a small town to redevelop an old building in a downtown that was also going through redevelopment. During this semester I asked students to read *A Creative Companion* and react to it in their journals and in the computer conference. I also began to introduce other books and exercises in class to explore the creative process and feelings about service in more depth. As concepts were discussed on the computer conference, students began to explore the spiritual dimension in their lives and their design processes.

One student reflected on a personal experience he had as a child that resulted in a creative flow of ideas. "It made me think of being eight years old and climbing the giant maple in front of a friend's house. We would climb until the limbs could not support us. It felt as though we were floating weightless above the neighborhood. We would hide from everyone, lost among the leaves. We had not a care in the world. After we came down from our tree-top oasis, we would play with blocks or in the sand box. Our creativity was explosive. Now, I feel like I need to find another 'tree' to climb. I know it's out there, I just need to start looking for it." This memory of positive conditions leading to creative thinking was important to this student's development of his ideas for the design project. In addition, other students who read this on the computer conference also began to share their personal experiences with creativity and what seemed to enhance it.

Another student wrote on the computer conference about her spiritual experience. "I spent over a year studying Zen Buddhist meditation and teachings. This included long retreats of silence and sitting meditation. Many Buddhists would argue that if you are not living in the present moment you are not experiencing life. True mindfullness (being in the present moment) is not just a cliche. It is a true state of being that is completely undervalued by American culture. Not only is one more able to access creativity in mindfulness, but compassion as well." At the time, this student was struggling with the stress of a group project where several of the students were unwilling to do a fair share of the work. In the past, this student would have quietly picked up others' tasks and completed them. In considering compassion for others, she began to discuss the reasons other students were having difficulty completing the work and found that encouraging and praising what they did finish resulted in more productivity within the group and more positive relations among group members. Her sharing of spiritual experiences also caused some group members to understand her better and improve their personal relations with her.

At this time I realized my own life was out of balance. I wrote in my journal, "Balance: I get angry because the proportion of things I do is not balanced for me. I am doing something for others and then not doing something for myself. I find it frustrating that I don't move closer to goals and seem to work hard constantly without reward." Part of a teacher's life involves placing others' needs over one's own, and I had not balanced that recently, letting others' needs too frequently take precedence over my career and personal needs.

However, by the end of the semester I was becoming more aware of the flow of life around me and through me as I was reading, writing, and thinking about how spirituality was part of my life and my approach to design. "Synchronicity," I noted in another entry. "I just had my second experience with it this month. My previous experiences with synchronicity were so long ago I can not now fully remember any of them." After examining the creative process in children during the past year as it influenced the creative process in design studios, I opened a design competition project for the winter 1998 semester to design a children's clothing store. "What a great opportunity! I am going to call my daughter's fourth grade teacher and ask if my design class can work with her elementary class as a team to develop the conceptual designs for the store. If you listen, you will hear what you need to hear."

The design of the children's clothing store was the focus, then, of a project in one of my design studio courses the following semester. Design students provided service to elementary students through visits to the school to work with them on the design process—a mutual learning experience— and through sharing information on college life and why they had chosen a career in design. Reflection and discussion continued on a computer journal as well as in private journals. Journal topics included reactions to classroom exercises and reactions to visits with the elementary school children. We were also able to have the children participate in our computer journal through the Internet connection in their classroom.

As the semester began, one exercise in class was developed to encourage students to use active methods to expand their creative processes and to encourage more discussion about the effects providing service to others had on students. Several books containing helpful or spiritual quotations were brought to studio and a quote from each was selected and read. I asked students to think about the quotes and write about them in the computer conference.

One student wrote, "The phrase I read was: 'If we keep doing what we're doing, we'll keep getting what we're getting.' This statement seems to supercede most of the others that we had to select from. It emphasizes that change must come from within before it shows on the outside and in our lives. If we wear ourselves down with negative thoughts, then negativity will burden our lives. If we think positive thoughts, then our lives will become a positive statement." This discussion early in the design process of the threat that negative thoughts can have on creative ideas was helpful to several students who said they sometimes fell into negative self-talk when they began to think about ideas for their designs.

Another student wrote on the computer conference: "The statement I chose is about 'practicing random acts of kindness.' I have found that it truly is better to give than receive and one can get so much from giving. If you are always looking at what you are going to receive from others you can never truly be happy with yourself. You need to give of yourself, your time, talents and treasures and in return I think you get much more." This affirmation of the positive aspects of service caused many of the students to focus on the service aspect of the elementary school visits. They considered the needs of the elementary students prior to their first visit and found that this increased awareness aided communication. Several of the college students found that having the elementary students play the role of experts on children's clothing stores freed the children to become very involved in the project.

During this semester students added discussion sessions to the computer conference that revealed aspects of their lives not usually shared in the classroom. A discussion about their pets was particularly interesting as each person shared feelings about their pets along with the usual photos and descriptions. When one of the student's cats died during the semester, it brought up things we usually don't confront in a design course. Some of these issues were important in the awareness several students began to have of the importance of life and the need to connect with one's inner self as well as with the lives or others. This increased inner awareness and ability to prioritize what was important helped some students expand their ideas for the design project.

Another discussion started by students was called "Thoughts, Wisdom and Sayings." People simply shared quotations that were relevant to them. About fifty quotations appeared during the semester and the flow was interesting given the common issues, problems, concerns and challenges that students were facing. One student offered a quote from Jean Paul Richter: "Why wait for extraordinary circumstances to do good? Use ordinary situations." This spoke to the discussions we had in class about providing service within the design profession and that even the small projects we did in class were important to others as well as ourselves. Another offering came from Eleanor Roosevelt: "You gain strength, courage, and confidence by every experience in which you really stop to look fear in the face. You must do the thing which you think you cannot do." This quotation came during the time when students were developing their initial ideas for their projects. Fear can be a major detriment to creative ideas, and this quote led to class discussion on what fears students had when they were developing their designs. Some feared that their ideas might not be taken seriously by others. Some students also feared that they could not develop a creative solution in the time available. Acknowledging these fears helped students develop strategies to deal with them in a positive way during the early phase of the design project.

"[T]o be nobody but yourself—in a world which is doing its best, night and day, to make you like everybody else—means to fight the hardest battle which any human being can fight, and never stop fighting." This quote by e.e. cummings also addresses the issue of creative design develop-ment and the struggle it can sometimes become. Many students try to gain acceptance for themselves and their ideas by doing what is expected and often find this approach does not result in a creative solution to a problem. Thinking about the fact that there are forces working to maintain a status quo that is comfortable for some people, allows students to realize that there is some struggle involved in developing new ideas and solutions to problems. This realization allowed several students in the class that semester to present more creative ideas with the understanding that everyone in class understood the struggle that this involves.

Students learned much from the experience with the elementary class. Several realized that fourth graders do not pay attention to a topic very long. The quick shift in thinking, however, allowed the elementary students to develop interesting ideas quickly. During the first meeting, many of the ele-mentary students developed several ideas for concepts for the stores. Their ideas were detailed and they did not seem constrained by worrying about whether what they wanted could really be built or not. A report by one student indicated that "We came up with aliens [as a theme] and what clothes aliens would wear. They drew me pictures of what aliens look like." This experience with the creative process in children was enlightening to many of the students in terms of some of the problems they were having with their own creative processes. The freedom from constraint that elementary students demonstrated in the initial idea stage of a project was important to the college students' recognition that they had limited their own creative potential by rejecting ideas too quickly because of perceived constraints.

The next visit to the elementary students included the design students' initial concepts presented in a graphic and three-dimensional form that could be experienced and commented on by the elementary students. This part of the project turned out to be the most creative work done by the design students during the semester, including several sculptural pieces and some interesting graphic collages illustrating the store theme presented.

During the first schematic review for the store design, the design students simplified their initial ideas because they were concerned about whether they could eventually produce drawings that would explain how to build their ideas, even though these types of drawings were not required at this stage of the project. Already, the creative aspects of the projects developed in the early stages were being discarded for what was comfortable and familiar. With encouragement, several design students did persist and developed innovative designs.

In my journal I recorded my observation of this process. "Creativity is still alive in fourth grade. It has not been squeezed out of them yet. The need to bring out creativity in design students is a constant challenge and one that I have grown with. I have had to push my own creative instincts to try to connect with the creative souls that are there but are often well hidden. This is the part of teaching design that I love."

At the end of each semester I survey my students to find out how effective they think the computer conference journal experience is. Sixty-five percent of the students in one design studio course found it effective while 35 percent preferred to write journals privately and did not use it. All of the students in studio found the creative thinking games played in class to be effective. Students in this course were also asked to record thoughts into a private journal daily (that would remain private) for two weeks during this class and about half found it effective (57 percent) and about half did not (43 percent).

Examination of data from pre-test and post-test surveys administered each semester reveals that most students develop a clearer understanding of spirituality during the semester. The interconnectedness of things is a common part of several students' descriptions of spirituality, and the importance of spirituality in their lives is also mentioned. Trust and a flow to things are mentioned several times, and one student remarked that she needed to connect with the spiritual throughout the day, not just when things are difficult. The need to find a calming ritual is important to several students' concepts of spirituality. The biggest change in perception of spirituality is that it is commonly defined as an aspect of organized religion at the beginning of the semester and by the end is considered in a broader context.

Most students' attitudes about service do not substantially change during the semester. Many students are already experienced with providing service to others and find it positive. Only one of my students did not plan to continue providing service to others in the future. All of the students are positive about the service they provide to the elementary class and appreciate this opportunity. The majority intend to continue providing service to others and several indicate their plans to render service during the summer such as building houses for Habitat for Humanity or working in local soup kitchens.

The journey I began in the fall of 1996 to integrate service into my teaching started with my search for awareness of the world around me and increased connection with my inner self so I could understand my own feelings about service and its role in my life and career. The first difficult lesson I learned is to let go. Once I have done this I am able to pay more attention to what is happening around me and within me. I then begin to trust and follow my instincts more often. I am better able to respond to opportunities that are part of an overall flow in my journey, beginning with the training and support I received from my university's service-learning center that led to the initial integration of service-learning into my teaching. After that, I continued to search for my inner self through many methods and became aware of the research on spirituality and health through a visit to the Fetzer Institute that focused on the architectural design of their facilities. Shortly after that visit I received a grant to integrate both spirituality and service-learning in my teaching and writing

I will continue on my journey to explore the integration of service-learning and spirituality in teaching design. My next project will consider spirituality and its influence on both the design process as well as the final design product. Research on spiritual traditions that influence sacred places and buildings will be the focus of a multi-disciplinary design studio course I am co-developing. The focus on place will expand beyond the more traditional definitions in architectural practice to a consideration of sacred places that are part of both the built environment as well as the natural world.

Community Service in Architecture and Urban Planning: Venues of Motivation and Satisfaction

Kurt Brandle and Nancy M. Wells

"**G**etting notoriously impractical architecture students into the real world is a revolution in itself." This comment by Amy Virshup, from a 1997 *New York Times Magazine* article, describes Auburn University's Rural Studio. Its director, Samuel Mockbee, is known in architectural education for his work with students creating homes for the rural poor of Alabama and for giving people the houses at no charge. The article's subtitle reads: "In a profession not known for its social conscience, the Rural Studio creates beautiful houses for clients who would be happy just to get running water." Virshup later quotes one professor's prediction that "[i]n three years, Habitat for Humanity will be the largest builder of affordable housing, while architects sit around debating the merits of deconstructionism."

It is true that the architecture and planning professions do not have a reputation as major providers of community service. Neither has community service traditionally been a significant part of the culture in architectural education. Yet articles like the one mentioned above and common public opinion underestimate the community service activities that occur within schools of architecture and urban planning and in the professions. Design centers, for example, have provided valuable services in poor urban areas over decades, usually involving schools of architecture and urban planning as well as professional volunteers. No doubt, service-learning activity is occurring around us. So, we decided to find out what was happening in the College of Architecture and Urban Planning at our school, the University of Michigan.

In the first part of our essay we look at the ways architects and planners work and how such work may relate to community service and service-learning. Then we report on what types of projects students and alumni of the College are involved in, what motivates people to get involved, and what satisfaction is derived from such involvement.

COMMUNITY SERVICE

Our work as architects and urban planners is often service oriented. We develop frameworks from which others can coordinate and build, be it the design and specification for schools and hospitals or the planning and guidelines of cities and regions. The central and implicit objective always is to find how we can facilitate human interaction and promote the welfare of people. While our task is usually to design or plan physical structures and infrastructures, or to provide the means for others to do so, our fundamental quest is toward comprehending human dimensions in the broadest possible sense. This involvement makes community service a strong force for personal growth in our profession—not one-way giving but service-learning during one's education and throughout a whole career. This means, even when we do "something for nothing" for the common good, we gain and gain rather substantially, and often very differently than from professional involvement for remuneration.

As in all of education, education in architecture and urban planning depends on learning-by-doing in order to test theories and build experience. Simulation of real world situations through physical and computer models, thought experiments, gaming, etc., is used to a large extent. Architecture and urban planning design studios and seminar settings are at the center of learning, with knowledge integrated from architectural history, building technology, and other related areas such as psychology, sociology, engineering, ecology and economics.

Such simulation is essentially also what happens everyday in the profession itself, however with the outlook and pressure for the implementation of designs and planning and with the benefit from such realization. In education, quasi feedback about implementation is available in the form of critiques from professors and peers. The observation of the translation, however, from design scheme to product outcome is missing. Also largely missing is the input from the clients which in praxis happens not only in the design development but also during the implementation process. Students who gain related experience during employment while still studying are very lucky as client interaction is usually not part of such intermittent work. But the experience is important as architecture and urban planning heavily depend on the interaction with clients for learning about their needs, desires, and limitations.

It is crucial to take into account these needs, desires, and limitations throughout the whole development of a project—the earlier the better, as decisions are increasingly difficult to revoke down-the-path, and late rather than early changes are nearly always more costly. Community service, usually with strong cost constraints, brings these criteria forward early and forcefully, and therefore brings high returns in the form of service-learning.

There are many opportunities for architects and urban planners to engage in community service, from simple to rather complicated work. We may use our muscles with a non-profit organization in framing, drywalling, or painting a house for a needy family. We may design a masterplan for a neighborhood to foster community interaction. We may analyze the economic viability of a site in a run-down area for production facilities, not least toward providing jobs. Such tasks range from the work simply requiring labor to the work requiring analytic and creative expertise.

Everything we do as architects and urban planners, except for very rudimentary work, involves in one way or another solving problems within complexity. Design and planning call for considering many aspects of problems simultaneously, in a dual mode of problem seeking and problem solving. The ability to work with complex problems can be especially helpful in community service. In return, community service can provide opportunities to acquire the insights and skills for work in complexity. There are two kinds of community service with many variations in between: first, help in accomplishing clearly defined work and, next, help in finding creative solutions in poorly defined situations. In general, these are not different from work in any other context. What is different in community service are the partners and their motivations, their ways of interaction and valuation, and how the expected outcomes influence the participants and their work.

It follows that community service rarely involves a simple relationship of providers, on one side, and recipients on the other. The definition of a problem at hand is already a task of cooperation. What must be done to address and to solve it will tend toward direct assistance or toward collaborative involvement, most situations requiring more or less of each. Direct assistance can satisfy a particular need for which the community does not have the capacity. For those who provide the service it involves activities in which they are qualified. Practitioners come with experience; students seek and should find it with their help.

Collaborative involvement requires much more. While the problem is identified in general, to grasp its underlying conditions and potential scope are a major part of the project. How the partners relate to each other comes into play, with social and educational differences as background. The potential for clash exists if differences are not recognized, discussed, and taken into account. Gaps in communication must be eliminated, and the effectiveness of communication methods must be explored early.

This early stage may well be the most sensitive period in the whole project. In their 1998 article "Learning from Difference," for example, Margaret Dewar and Claudia Isaac note that student learning through community service in Detroit "has exposed a major clash of culture between the university way of operating and the way community organizations function." Community organizations typically function very differently from academic institutions or professional enterprises with inherently other ways of thinking and decision making. Individuals must step up to mediate, hopefully from both sides. Here is the central role for experienced faculty members, architects or planners, and community leaders. "Sensitive openness" may be the best characterization of what is called for. It may relate to social, economic, ethnic, environmental or technical issues. Guidance to learning and acting jointly are the crucial objectives.

The approach and process of problem solving may at times be more assistance-driven, at other times more community-driven, depending on the dynamics of progress, the input of expertise and the feedback from the community partner. At best, all participants see themselves as community builders.

The primary objective of education in universities and colleges is to prepare students for professional work in a chosen field. As important, but not as prominent, is a general education toward understanding current social, economic and political issues. While community service nearly always deals in one way or another with both components, higher education does not sufficiently address their interrelationship. There are now strong indications of change and many institutions have recently developed programs for service-learning through community involvement.

The Mission Statement of the College of Architecture and Urban Planning at the University of Michigan provides the background for all academic activities. It reads, in part: "The condition of humanity is intimately connected to the environment in which we live. Accordingly, the primary mission of the College is to prepare students for positions of responsibility within a wide spectrum of organizations and institutions whose goals are to improve the quality of our lives and environment. . . . The College fosters creative links among its programs in teaching, research, scholarship, and outreach."

From this statement and earlier remarks there should be little doubt that well-developed service-learning activities enrich curricula. However, the only course dedicated to community service in our College is called Integrative Field Experience in the Urban and Regional Planning Program, a class providing "a two-term capstone experience involving second-year students working directly with community-based organizations in urban neigh-

borhoods and planning districts in Detroit." There are several courses in the
College that from time to time use community service fully or partially as
the means to expose students to real world problems. Some of the more
recent projects include design and work on the construction site for low-
income housing, design and building of stage sets for a community theatre,
development of urban design proposals for inner city neighborhoods and
waterfronts, and studies on energy efficient, affordable housing units.

The variety of these projects illustrates that community service-learning can occur in a wide range of educational settings. The results from our
student and alumni surveys point to the positive experiences such service
yields for personal and professional growth. Therefore, we may conclude
that every student, especially at the graduate level, should be required to
participate in a community service project and that related course offerings
should be available on a regular basis.

RESULTS FROM A STUDENT AND ALUMNI SURVEY

During the spring and summer of 1998, we distributed nearly identical surveys to present and former students of the College of Architecture and
Urban Planning in order to learn about their experiences with community
service projects. The in-house survey went to 400 people, nearly all the students who were currently enrolled. Sixty-one students replied, representing a
14 percent response rate. The alumni survey was more targeted, with distribution to individuals known or thought to have had community service
involvement. Twenty-nine people replied, a yield of 29 percent of the surveys sent out.

Survey respondents were asked to indicate the general topic(s) of their
community service involvement from a list of six issues. Given the nature of

the architecture and urban planning professions as well as the character of current social problems, it is not surprising that the most common service of students was related to housing and homelessness and, for alumni, economic and community development. "Other" service topics listed by students include working with the elderly, developing alcohol awareness programs, and community organizing. For alumni, the "other" services include participating in youth programs, political campaigns, and religious work.

Types of Community Service Involvement of Students and Alumni

STUDENTS	ALUMNI
Housing / Homelessness	Economic / Community / Development
Economic / Community Development	Housing / Homelessness
Other	Teaching / Mentoring
Teaching / Mentoring	Energy Conservation / Environmentalism
Energy Conservation / Environmentalism	Other
Gender Issues	Gender Issues

Answers to a question about when people got involved show that 85 percent of the students who responded to the survey had their first community service involvement before and 15 percent had their first involvement while studying at the College. Of the alumni, 74 percent had their first community service involvement before, 7 percent during, and 14 percent after being at the College. These findings are consistent with research by Alexander Astin and colleagues in 1991, who report that 63 percent of college students active in community service began their involvement while in high school or earlier.

Considerable research attention has focused on the motivations or decision factors that lead people to volunteerism or community service. Of the more than 700 students surveyed by Robert Serow in 1991, the "sense of satisfaction from helping others" was mentioned as a deciding factor by 80 percent of the respondents. In his report, "Students and Volunteerism," Serow lists other motivations for service mentioned by a substantial percentage of students, including "Involve[ment] through club, activity or class," "duty to correct societal problems," "meeting people," "acquiring career skills and experience," and "attraction of the work itself." These responses reflect the classic motivational themes of volunteerism that are described in the literature. In a 1987 article about "Characteristics and Motivations of College Students Volunteering for Community Service," Thomas Fitch suggests that three categories best capture these motivations: altruistic, egoistic (or self-interested), and social obligation.

The same themes are apparent in our survey of students' motivations. As shown in the following table, the most highly rated items reflect, in the main, altruistic motivations. Of the top five, only "To learn something new" strongly reflects self-interest motivation. Note that although 88 percent of the respondents indicated that their community service project was arranged by a professor, "required for class" is seventh of the 12 reasons for participation, suggesting that other motivations clearly outweigh the class obligation.

While the more "self-interest" oriented motivations are not, in general, rated as high as the altruistic ones, these data nevertheless suggest that self-interest factors do play a motivating role in community service. Such "selfish" motives warrant further attention. Within the context of promoting environmentally responsible behavior, Kearney, Kaplan, and DeYoung—in "Some Psychological Aspects of Altruism and Self-Interest," a paper given at the Western Psychological Association's 77th Annual Convention—convincingly argue that while altruism may be a necessary motive in the promotion of environmentally sensitive behavior, it is not always sufficient.

Motivations for Community Service (1 = not at all, 5 = a great deal)

	STUDENTS	ALUMNI	OVERALL
To contribute to a better society	4.15	4.48	4.26
It's a worthwhile activity	4.10	4.45	4.21
To learn something new	3.90	3.62	3.81
It's the right thing to do	3.44	4.17	3.68
To give something back	3.33	4.17	3.60
To gain professional skills	3.28	3.10	3.22
To learn about myself	2.28	3.03	2.89
To meet new people	2.64	3.03	2.77
Required for class	2.98	1.23	2.46
To have fun with friends	2.52	2.21	2.43
To make professional connections	2.10	2.59	2.26
To put on my résumé	2.13	2.00	2.09

Altruism is not the only "legitimate" motivation for behavior. These authors debunk the myth that only "good" motives lead to "good" outcomes, and point out that there are many self-interest-based reasons for wanting to preserve the planet. The same can be said for many types of community service. Much of the community service literature indicates that individuals often receive personal benefit from improving a neighborhood, fighting suburban sprawl, or picking up trash. Kearney and her colleagues go on to say that "bad" (i.e., self-interest) motives are not in opposition to "good" (i.e., altruistic) motives. Rather, they argue, multiple motives come into play in determining behavior and ought to be recognized and embraced in the promotion of environmentally or socially beneficial behaviors.

Furthermore, Michael Frisch and Meg Gerrard found in a 1981 survey that self-oriented motives (such as "career exploration and development" and "learn[ing] how to relate to people") are particularly important for young volunteers. In "Natural Helping Systems," they state: "It is important to recognize the role that personal growth and fulfillment, as opposed to self-sacrifice, plays in the motives of younger volunteers." In their 1993 study of AIDS volunteers, Allen Omoto and his colleagues found that individuals whose motivation for volunteering is more self-oriented, rather than primarily altruistic, are more likely to continue volunteering for many years, thus exhibiting more durable behavior. Writing in *The Social Psychology of HIV Infection*, they state: "Continuing volunteers can be distinguished from quitters not . . . by their community concern and humanitarian values . . . but by their greater 'selfish' desires to feel good about themselves and to learn more about AIDS." Clearly, self-oriented motivations are valuable and legitimate reasons for community service and ought not to be minimized or discouraged.

OUTCOMES OF THE COMMUNITY SERVICE EXPERIENCE

Respondents in our survey were also asked about the outcomes of their community service experience. Students responded to the following question: "to what extent have the following been outcomes of your community service experience?"

In general, these responses suggest a high level of satisfaction with the community service experience. Furthermore, when asked "Would you recommend that others participate in a similar type of community service project?" the mean response was 4.36 for students and 4.81 for alumni, indicating participants must have derived a great deal from their experience.

Many comments in the narrative sections of the survey point to the advantages of community service by seeing tangible outcomes of efforts, working with organizations, and thinking about career directions. Some of the negative comments can help to avoid pitfalls and can help to reshape service-learning programs.

Outcomes of the Community Service Experience (1 = not at all, 5 = a great deal)

	STUDENTS	ALUMNI
I will be more likely volunteer in the future	4.02	3.90
Community service has opened my eyes to broad social and cultural issues	3.67	4.10
Community service has influenced my career	3.25	3.76
Community service has become a part of my life	3.05	4.07

The following paraphrased expressions indicate satisfaction from service-learning by students: giving something back to the community; making a difference; seeing recipients happy; having opportunities to practice skills; working with dedicated citizens; seeing tangible outcomes; learning about cooperation in a larger group; and learning about building in practice. The following samples indicate problems: scheduling conflicts with other course work; lack of time to participate fully; insufficient planning of service activities; and too much time taken for logistics.

A few positive and negative experiences by faculty members reinforce students' comments. Some faculty cited, for example, satisfaction in seeing a studio have an impact beyond its own pedagogical objective and seeing students grow in their understanding of real world community activities and needs. Others noted lack of access to project information along with inefficiency and slowness of community leaders to respond.

Looking back to their service-learning experience and considering their present involvement alumni wrote comments like "it has broadened my horizon, professionally and personally" and "it also allowed me to gain useful insights into specific career paths"; "it has given me visibility in the larger community that I would not have enjoyed through my paid position alone"; "I have become more sensitive to the ways in which issues of social and economic justice are physically manifest in the environment and environmental design"; "it put into perspective that some things must be done without regard to price or money"; "although it was not my initial intent, I have found many clients for my practice through contacts made while volunteering"; "it provides an exposure to politics as an implementation tool."

CONCLUSION

Many students considered seeing the outcomes of what they designed as one of the most satisfying aspects of community service—that is, seeing material manifestations of ideas and constructs, even in simple, down-to-earth situations. Such experiences are crucial for the maturing process of personal and professional responsibility in fields that are so oriented toward tangible results as architectural design and urban planning. The further we come in our professional journey, the more we understand that learning from outcomes is never ending, and we are often surprised by what evolved from what we imagined.

We are, in all of our daily life, perhaps most consciously engaged in community service, alternating between modes of self-interest and altruism. This is essentially how in the broadest context humanity thrives, moves on, and endures. It is through affiliation that self-interest and altruism are activated, come into focus, and develop toward differentiation and fruition. Fundamental implications for design and planning professionals are emerging in our age of radical capitalism and consumerism, with the inevitable prospect of work time reduction. Community service may grow in relation to increased leisure time and provide meaningful activities, as suggested by Jeremy Rifkin in *The End of Work*. The creation of environments that facilitate new community life will be largely the task of architects and urban planners. Community service is an important activity to understand community life and gain insight into how to design for it.

The Roads Mistaken

David D. Cooper

My title is cribbed from Robert Frost's much-read and often-misunderstood poem "The Road Not Taken." In it, Frost imagines himself somewhere deep in the woods, slightly confused and disoriented, facing a fork in a road. The traveler's predicament inspires some of the most popular and enigmatic lines in modern American poetry. Should he take the road that shows more wear, the one where other travelers have safely passed before him—the path, perhaps, of least resistance? Or should he choose the other route, the one that is grassy and lacks wear? Eventually, he selects the less-worn path. Choose your own road, Frost seems to be saying. Make your own way. Resist the seductions of conformity. Go where no one—or very few fellow travelers— has dared to go before.

The only hitch is that the road Frost eventually chooses is really "just as fair," he demurs in an important aside, as the one he doesn't choose. Besides, that particular morning each path "equally lay / In leaves no step had trodden black." If the poem is about the importance of taking less popular paths, why did Frost confuse the issue with the title "The Road *Not* Taken"? Could it be that the journeys of our lives have less to do with the actual choices we make when confronted by options and turning points? And much more with our interpretations of the decisions we make, along with the perceptions others make of our choices? Or is the traveler's topographical predicament an analog for the journey of the inner life? Is making sense of the roads we travel, then, an *inside job*? What matters most for Frost may not in fact be the paths themselves, and certainly not the starkly diverging directions each lures him to take. What matters is how he will look back on his choices years later and see what difference *he* made *of* them and not what difference *they* made *in* him.

> I shall be saying this with a sigh
> Somewhere ages and ages hence:
> Two roads diverged in a wood, and I—
> I took the one less traveled by,
> And that has made all the difference.

In many ways this essay is written with just such a sigh, for I too will be looking back, trying to make some sense of the roads I have traveled. When I do, I often see myself, like many other academics of my generation, facing hurdles, hitting roadblocks, or wandering up cul de sacs. Most higher education faculty, myself included, eventually face the same pseudo-predicament as Frost's traveler. At some point in our careers we face forks in the road. One route, well paved and maintained, points to scholarship and research. Another leads to teaching. Bending to the underbrush, a third path, faintly worn, fades off into service. In spite of institutional rituals and appointment, promotion, and tenure bylaws to the contrary, these routes remain, for most intents and purposes, separate pathways. Like Frost's traveler, faculty make their choices and stick to their career paths, "knowing how way leads to way" and doubting "if I shall ever come back" to take a different route.

Given this dominant and polarizing three-tiered model of research, teaching, and service, no wonder some faculty lead fractured lives, unable to achieve wholeness, self-renewal, and a sense of authenticity that form the spiritual ground of an integrated life. Instead, we enter into separate and isolated formations. We choose the professional career life of disciplinary specialization and theoretical abstraction that often rewards self-enclosure and retreat into private space. Or we opt for the institutional life of teaching lived out on the intellectual commons of our colleges and universities where the values of collegiality and tradition are supposed to countervail excesses of disciplinary specialization. Or we engage the ethical life of service that brings us to the intersection of career and the larger public sphere where we find ourselves, as Martin Luther King, Jr. put it, "caught in an inescapable network of mutuality, tied into a single garment of destiny" with others who share our place and time.

More and more faculty today experience academic life as a tension between these formations. As a consequence, faculty, staff, and even students, I have learned from dialogues with educators across America, are articulating a resounding sense of disconnectedness, isolation, and a lack of authenticity from one another, their institutions, society and within themselves. That disconnectedness is especially acute among humanities faculty who seem trapped into a rhetoric of difference. Even the very word "common," notes distinguished literary critic and Yale educator David Bromwich, "is subject to a delicate prohibition" in the discourse of contemporary humanists.

The good news is that this sense of existential and spiritual fracture arises, I believe, out of what might be called the "automyth" of research-teaching-service. An "automyth" is something we believe in *only* because we do not believe in anything else. Like Frost's traveler, it is not the automyths we act out, but the myths we *live* that matter most to an integrated life. Likewise, it is not the paths we take but what we make of them during the journey that counts. In the case of academics, why can't we redirect our scholarship, for example, into lives of meaningful service? Or refashion our service into highly reputable scholarship? And transform our teaching into both? These alternative configurations challenge the prevailing academic automyth. They rest at the core of my following reflections on scholarship, teaching, and service and the currents of autobiography that flow, sometimes invisibly, through each of them, forming the confluence of a more integrated learning life.

I want to offer my own story as an exploratory narrative of personal and professional struggle toward wholeness, authenticity, and self-renewal with respect to merging the pathways of profession, community, and the inner life. I do not consider my own academic career or, indeed, my spiritual journey, in any sense exemplary or, to be sure, worthy of emulation. My story may bring some light, however, to important questions: Can faculty bring their "whole selves" to their work in higher education? Can scholarship forge strong and meaningful links to the inner life? What do scholarship, teaching, and service look like when they support authenticity, wholeness, and spiritual renewal? Two chapters in my unfolding academic journey, in particular, may be viable explorations that bridge the inner life of mind and spirit with the active life of social action: my writing on Thomas Merton and my embrace, years later, of service-learning pedagogy and philosophy.

Nearly ten years ago, I published a controversial book on the monk, poet, and social critic Thomas Merton. I engaged Merton's extraordinary spiritual and literary journey by tracking his inner conflicts, self-doubts, and ambivalences—a crucible of creative inner tensions that is the wellspring, I argued, of Merton's important message for our own troubled times. Little did I know at the time that in charting Thomas Merton's journey I was surveying my own pathway through identity confusion and vocational crisis into self-acceptance, personal integrity, greater spiritual resilience, and hunger for ultimate concerns.

In a "Speculative Epilogue" to that book, I tried to retrace Thomas Merton's story using the psychoanalyst Erik Erikson's pioneering work on moral development and identity formation. I discovered that the broad outlines of the Merton biography bear marked and interesting similarities to Erikson's eight stages of identity development. I was especially drawn to the crucial and pivotal period he called the early adulthood identity crisis—a term that has become, unfortunately, much clichéd since Erikson coined it in the 1950s. In his revealing psychological biographies of Martin Luther and Mohandas Gandhi, for example, Erikson focuses on their mid-life turmoils. He argues that this period of isolation, withdrawal, and critical inner searching holds the key to understanding the dynamic processes of confused and conflicted young persons successfully negotiating the journey into mature and responsible adulthood. Through his psychoanalytic work, Erikson found that identity conflicts flare up and seek resolution during an identity moratorium of early adulthood. Those conflicts eventually pave the way to living the remaining developmental stages of life unified and reconciled. One is better equipped, Erikson felt, to accept oneself and to embrace with less resignation and ambivalence one's place in society. The mid-life identity crisis, in short, shapes and tempers a lasting and durable sense of adult duty. Once resolved, according to Erikson, an individual is ready to engage the balance of the life course with social commitment, caring, personal integrity and trust.

Erikson warns, however, that the identity crisis cannot be resolved by building an adult personality on one's most desirable persona and projecting what he called "negative identity fragments" upon the world or other people. In retelling Thomas Merton's story in Erikson's terms, I argued that this seems to be precisely what Merton had persisted in doing during his tumultuous and vulnerable thirties. The period spanned Merton's early years in a Trappist monastery, from roughly 1946—when he was writing his best selling autobiography *The Seven Storey Mountain*—to the mid 1950s. During this time Merton repeatedly projected his negative identity as a writer and poet onto what he made out to be a profane and hostile secular world. Meanwhile, he took shelter in a positive and idealized role identification as a contemplative monk. This pattern of identity conflict forms the dominant theme of Merton's poetry and autobiographical writing during the 1940s and early 1950s.

Merton himself eventually came to realize, as he writes in a journal that breaks new ground in the late 1950s, that "a personal crisis is creative and salutary [only] if one can accept the conflict and restore unity on a higher level, incorporating the opposed elements in a higher unity. One thus becomes a more complete, a more developed person. . . ." For Merton, this meant that he had to make peace with his self-image as a writer and no longer expel that self-image as a worldly and secular toxin to his contemplative life. Erik Erikson considers that process of self-acceptance as the end-game, so to speak, of identity formation. It gives rise to an authentic self-awareness from which an individual can travel the future life course, Erikson concludes, emboldened by integrity, a renewed capacity for intimacy with others, and, above all, a heightened obligation to lead and guide subsequent generations, a quality Erikson refers to as "generativity." I maintain throughout my book that Merton's decade-long crisis of identity confusion gradually nourished what Erikson might have predicted: namely, a wisdom to care in entirely news ways for persons and institutions, an extraordinary capacity for ultimate concerns, and a redoubled dedication of his writing to the moral and ethical maintenance of the human condition in his time. I even claim that he became a better institutional citizen—that is to say, a better Trappist monk whose spiritual needs were further served by embracing the self-identity of a writer whom Merton once disparaged as "a traitor in my Trappist mornings."

In the closing paragraph of the book, I suggested that there may be no better way to evaluate Merton's legacy than what is implied in Erik Erikson's capstone virtue of generativity. He frames that virtue as an existential assertion: "I am what survives of me." That declaration, I believe, is the inspirational thread that runs through Thomas Merton's prodigious outpouring of letters, poems, essays and books written after his identity moratorium. The extent of his generative commitment is nowhere stated with greater clarity and simplicity than in his comment to a teenage correspondent (Merton's source for the latest rock-and-roll releases). In a letter to her, he declares that they must work together to make the world a better place, to leave it in better shape than they had found it. On the occasion of his correspondent's graduation from high school, and just six months before his untimely and tragic accidental death in Bangkok, one generation addresses the other. Merton's advice: "Go forth into the world and help it, if possible, make some kind of sense. Or anyway less nonsense." I closed the Epilogue with a simple, unacademic claim: "Against that standard, Thomas Merton measured up."

Standing now on the threshold of my fiftieth birthday, the wisdom and clarity of hindsight reveals an insight that I was not prepared to see during my mid-thirties when I was writing the Merton book. Simply put, in writing Thomas Merton's story I was entering, albeit in a subliminal way, into my own journey, trying to make sense of my inner conflicts while I was engaging Merton's mid-life crisis. The demographic parallels are obvious. I was drawn to archival-level research on Thomas Merton's life and work during my mid-twenties, roughly the same age as Merton when he disappeared into a monastery tucked deeply into the Kentucky woods and began work on his autobiography, a period of unrelenting self-denial, intense self-scrutiny, and agonizing self-doubt. Returning to the manuscript sporadically during the next few years, the book was finally published in the late 80s when I was about the same age as Merton was when he broke through his mid-life identity crisis. The autobiographical similarities are less obvious but nonetheless painfully clear to me. I started a teaching career at the same time I began the Merton research in earnest, a couple years out of graduate school. During the next few years I watched my personal and professional life slump into a nose dive. Eventually, at the age of 40 I found renewal and reprieve in a new teaching job that set my life on a different course not unlike what Merton himself, at age 40, described as the salutary and creative outcome of a personal crisis.

Looking back now, I can easily recast the autobiographical details into the same Eriksonian terms I used then to tell Merton's story in the Epilogue.

Given the depressed conditions of the academic job market in the late 1970s, I began my first teaching job on a shoe string contract as a visiting lecturer in the English Department at a large public university. Even though my contract was renewed annually for several years, I remained cut off, it became clear to me from the outset of my appointment, from any hope of ever entering into the tenure system. I would never become a full institutional citizen and peer among the mostly older tenured faculty in the department and the very few lucky younger ones who had somehow slipped into the tenure stream right out of graduate school. Besides, I carried with me a deep and inchoate suspicion of academic culture. I was beginning to suffer acute ambivalence over what I had gotten myself into, especially the nagging realization that the future was not likely to measure up to an idealized version of the intellectual life that I had conjured early on in graduate school at an Ivy League university. In any event, my inner world soon began to look very much like the one I was writing about with increasing intensity and passion as I plotted out an Eriksonian mapping of Thomas Merton's mid-life identity crisis. Something important, of course, is lost in the retrospective clinical application of Erikson's psychoanalytic terms. Nonetheless, I see clearly now that I had begun to project my negative identity as a would-be academic and scholar onto a hostile and unforgiving university. My attitudes toward senior faculty began to sour into suspicion and disrespect. I grew cynical over the aims of university administrators whom I jokingly dismissed as "suits." I viewed my tenurable peers as young emperors without clothes. I soon joined a cadre of other temporary faculty. We harnessed our collective anger, organized a labor union, and agitated for reform. The fears and uncertainties I harbored over my future were redirected into a loathing for tenured faculty and university administrators who were quite comfortable, I was convinced, balancing their own security, empowerment, and status onto the bent backs of hard working, exploited, and disenfranchised part-time teachers.

In the meantime, I took flight into a positive and inflated role identification as a teacher and a writer. I wrote like a demon—on Thomas Merton and other American writers (mostly angry expatriates whose cultural disaffection appealed to me) along with interdisciplinary essays and articles on religion, film, teaching, and psychology. I developed new curricula and practiced teaching methods that were controversial, counter to mainstream, even subversive. I continued to devote myself with nervous intensity to teaching, writing, and cultivating self-righteous animosity toward The Suits until the tensions spilled over into a pervasive daily anxiety and internal division from which I found it more and more impossible to escape.

The unfortunate up-shot was that I became a self-enclosed teacher cut off from any understanding of my students' needs, incapable of exercising the critical empathy and emotional literacy that are a teacher's greatest tools. As a writer, I took on a pugnacious manner that my former dissertation director summarized in two blunt words: "prickly" and "pissed off." The department chair summoned me to his office on more than one occasion to reprimand me over reports of my aggressive behavior in the classroom and my superior attitude. I remember being dumbfounded by his claims. They struck me as impossible to understand in light of my great passion for teaching and my self-styled role as doormat and waterboy for the English Department. I had become, in truth, a perfectly obnoxious and deeply conflicted colleague. I earned a reputation for circulating righteous and accusatory rumors about the motives and hidden agendas of department and university administrators—all carried out in the name, of course, of tough and savvy political leadership on behalf of the union. I spiraled daily into fantasies that oscillated, often unpredictably, between visions of how much I loved my students and scenarios of how much I despised my

colleagues. These emotional conflicts usually culminated in a battle plan for
the next day's march to the front lines of my little war. In reality, I was only
grooming myself as a perfect candidate for dismissal from a lectureship that
I was lucky enough to hang onto for ten years.

In retrospect, that difficult decade comprises what Erik Erikson understood as an interval of often-exaggerated role experimentation, a "psychosocial moratorium," in Erikson's technical words, when an individual must
reconcile the often conflicting tasks of settling on an authentic self-image
while finding a niche in society. "A moratorium," Erikson writes, "is a
period of delay granted to somebody who is not ready to meet an obligation. . . . By psychosocial moratorium, then, we mean a delay of adult commitments [which] also often leads to deep, if often transitory, commitment."
This enthusiastic embrace of a transitory identity, Erikson further maintains,
frequently accompanies an excited, reactionary, even militant rejection of
contrary role identifications. Individuals so deeply committed, he says, "may
learn only much later that what [they] took so seriously was only a period
of transition." They may come to feel estranged from a self-image which
once seemed so firmly and uniquely suited to them. During this pivotal
stage of identity formation, "any experimentation with identity images,"
Erikson continues, "means also to play with the inner fire of emotions and
drives and to risk the outer damage of ending up in a social 'pocket' from
which there is no return."

I was blessed with the great gift of being guided through that moratorium by Thomas Merton. By following him into the inner fire of his own
psychosocial moratorium and engaging his struggle through my writing and
research, he served, in effect, as a pilot who helped navigate my parallel
inner journey through the shoals and rough waters of mid-life crisis. The
institutional alienation and collegial dislocation I felt during that period cer-

tainly extracted a serious toll on my professional, personal, and moral life. And I came away with a residual skepticism over academic culture that, to this day, wells up on occasion and forces me to practice patience and restraint and seek the counsel of trusted colleagues, old mentors, intimates, and friends. But in spite of the difficult straits I found myself in during my turbulent 30s, nothing succeeded in undermining my basic commitment to writing about Thomas Merton and his struggles to find what he called a "quiet but articulate place" where he too could fit in and carry on his life's work. In return for the emotional and intellectual energy I invested in the Merton book, I found gratification and a sense of inner direction and fulfillment that compensated for—indeed, rescued me from—the unhappiness and futility of my daily life at the university. Looking back, I can appreciate the wisdom of Erik Erikson's claim that during the identity crisis certain individuals dramatize their own crises by projecting them onto creative models of resolution. Among them, Erikson writes, are "works of art or . . . original deeds" spun by individuals "eager to tell us all about [their crises] in diaries, letters, and self-representations" or, for me, through biographical narrative. "[E]ven as the neuroses of a given period reflect the ever-present chaos of [a person's] existence . . . , the creative crises point to the period's unique solutions."

In my not remarkable case, the solutions were, in part, made for me when I was dismissed from my lectureship and found myself back in the chaotic academic marketplace looking for work. I applied for a million teaching positions. As good fortune would have it, I landed one temporary two-year instructorship. I was later hired into a tenure system appointment at the same university. It would be a mistake, however, to conclude that my professional renewal or emotional survival hinged solely on securing security of employment. An inner revolution was also taking place, spurred by ten years of identity confusion, role conflicts, and the inflated self-consciousness that comes from feelings of inferiority and self-doubt. Granted a new beginning, my identity confusion gradually gave way to renewed purposefulness. Once completely estranged from institutions, colleagues, and students, I began to feel a pull of intimacy and belonging toward my new university. Integrity slowly replaced despair. An obsession with justice and fair treatment receded against a new awareness of and appreciation for the workings of mercy in my life. Promise and possibility appeared on a spiritual horizon once edged by dark feelings of stagnation and entrapment.

I emerged from the Merton scholarship just as Merton had emerged from his psychosocial moratorium: with a powerfully renewed generative commitment and a much greater capacity and need for intimacy with others. More specifically, two new coordinates set the trajectory of my changing commitments as a teacher/scholar. First, the role that institutions play in shaping my identity and integrity became more important and obvious. While it is true that institutions sometimes betray us through rejection and, worse, indifference, they can also be, I sensed for the first time, important sources of affirmation, acceptance, and individuation. Second, a unitive spiritual and moral impulse began to inform and shape my intellectual and pedagogical work.

Once I had managed through the negative identity fragments I earlier projected onto the university, I began to realize that a life—especially a *teaching* life—lived outside of or free from the influence of institutions was more of an impoverishment than a virtue. Institutions of higher learning, by their very nature, shape us in profound ways. Without the strength and spirit of learning institutions pervading, as Erikson says, "patterns of care, . . . love, instruction and training, no strength could emerge from the sequence of generations. . . . From the stages of life, then, such dispositions as faith, will power, purposefulness, competence, fidelity, love, care, wisdom—all criteria of vital individual strength—*also flow into the life of institutions*. Without them," he warns, "institutions wilt" (the emphasis is mine). For my part, I struggled, sometimes against strong currents stirred by old animosities, to become a better institutional citizen. I recognized the reciprocity, as Erikson implies, between my individual strength and the larger mission and health of the public university that now employed me. I took on committee work, tentatively at first. I threw myself back into curricular innovation. Only this time I shaped courses and learning projects that were consonant with the core values of my new university and not, as my teaching experiments of the past, subversive and transparently anti-establishment. I even answered the call of academic service and took a temporary assignment as a program administrator, coming full circle from my old attitude toward academic administrators as rapacious, insensitive, ignorant, and self serving.

More important, a harmonic drive began to pervade my calling as a teacher, my intellectual interests and world view, as well as my philosophical inclinations. It was as if a new compass plotted my sense of moral direction. I became compelled to see the world around me and my place in it as a complex network of connections, integrations, balances, couplings, and ties that bind, and not a place of chaos, division, irreconcilable differences, and movement against the grain. Edward O. Wilson has recently jump-started an old philosophical term to describe this condition: underlying all forms of knowledge and ways of knowing is an urge to unity called "consilience." My new passion for connectivity went far beyond epistemology, however, and spilled over into an ecological lucidity that brought moral fluency across all sorts of boundaries. My teaching, in particular, fell under the influence of what Parker Palmer considers one of a teacher's greatest gifts,

"a capacity for connectedness." The challenge and the burden of the classroom became, in Palmer's choice words, "to weave a complex web of connection" between myself, my subject, my students, and eventually my
community "so that students can learn to weave a world for themselves . . .
The connections made by [such] teachers," Palmer wisely notes, "are not
held in their methods but in their hearts—meaning heart in its ancient sense,
as the place where intellect and emotion and spirit and will converge in the
human self."

These two guiding forces—the call of institutional citizenship and an
integrative impulse that forms the moral gravity of my world view—have
become the latitude and longitude of my current working life. As such, they
have brought me into the national service-learning movement while ushering
me out of the contemporary humanities.

The passion for convergence, I should briefly explain, sets me at odds
against a new generation of academics who have recently redefined the
humanities agenda. While many academic fields are striving toward a
vocabulary of disciplinary consilience, most Humanities disciplines have
taken a sharp opposite turn into postmodernism. Especially attractive are its
explicit prohibitions against universal truths, its skepticism over all claims
for connectivity and consensus, and its rejection of an enlightenment discourse of "spirit," "heart," "will," and "human self"—a vocabulary, as one
critic has it, that "reeks of the rotting carcass of liberal humanism." The
strong ideological position staked out in new humanities subfields like cultural, ethnic, and women's studies and bolstered by a related curriculum
reform movement inspired by hard-line multiculturalism are heavily colored
by postmodern skepticism over the possibilities for integration and consilience. For many of my younger colleagues, in particular, the democratic
ties that bind individual lives to the common welfare are now viewed,

through the skeptical lens of postmodernism, as political shackles that oppress. A shared body of moral values that integrates a curriculum into a social order threatens to become, we are warned, a pretense for domination by privileged classes and groups. Moreover, an interdisciplinary curriculum that aims for balance, commonality, and synthesis, according to postmodern pedagogy, is really no different than a curriculum that seeks to eradicate differences, thereby reinforcing ethnocentrism, cultural hegemony, and class oppression. Just at the same time, then, as my own academic work and teaching life broke through into a new set of commitments to transcend difference and seek common ground with others, my humanities colleagues were becoming far less concerned with the spirit of integration. They were much more preoccupied with ideology, identity politics, and the anxieties of the academic culture wars. Having emerged from the throes of personal crisis, I was bent on nourishing the fragile bond between the inner life and ethical responsibility to work, institution, and community—the essence, I believe, of a humanities education. Meanwhile, the disciplinary venue where I was situated to carry out my new work had become mental, abstract, contentious, and theory-driven.

About half of my writing during the past five years results from this friction between my renewed humanistic commitments and the contemporary humanities agenda. It is perhaps a new version of the old conflict I suffered during my 30s with another institutional status quo. If so, I hope it is as creative and salutary. But I hope too that it is less marred by anger and righteousness. To be sure, my last few essays and most recent book have been infused with considerable disappointment and discouragement. If I have been angry, I have tried to rechannel my anger, though, more positively and constructively or at least apply it more humbly and less derisively. In many ways my quarrel with the contemporary humanities has invigorated my commitments with important questions. How, for example, can I renew my own writing with the capacities and qualities of humanistic inquiry that I profess theoretically and defend in the abstract? How can I learn to teach and write with moral clarity, integrity, authenticity, and heart in an intellectual climate that is much too cerebral, too much *in the head*? Where can I find a community of fellow practitioners for whom the inner life, ethical commitment, and generative responsibility are central to career and not objects of derision or signs of philosophical bad faith? How can I find my way to common work in the university with its intellectual climate clouded by suspicion over consensus, commonality, and community?

Such questions have drawn me to service-learning pedagogy and philosophy. As I stated earlier, I emerged from the Merton scholarship with a renewed generative commitment and a greater capacity and need to build connections with others. I was also looking for ways to integrate what struck me as an artificial and even hypocritical division of academic life into the separate boxes of scholarship, teaching, and service. I was especially eager to explore avenues of service and find ways of becoming a participant in community and not, as I had been virtually my whole life, a spectator and critic quick to point out the failings and shortcomings of social life from my self-imposed vantage point, safely on the societal fringes. In addition to suiting up for community life, I wanted to integrate practices of service back into teaching and scholarship. Like most academics, however, I lacked a vehicle through which I could transform my teaching and scholarship into concrete expressions of social and moral action. *How could I be of service?* Now that I had gained a foothold on career security, I also lacked a model I could apply to integrate the professional pathways of teaching, research, and service. I found that vehicle and that model in service-learning.

Service-learning has had a cathartic effect on me far beyond its principal role as a community-responsive educational undertaking. It spins a much more complicated web. Service-learning ostensibly involves a set of teaching practices and experiential learning techniques that yoke together academic learning and students' active engagement with often-underserved groups in their communities; its aim is to promote students' moral, civic, and cognitive development, and pique their sense of social justice. But service-learning also carries with it strong philosophical currents, intellectual soundings, epistemological implications, interdisciplinary configurations, moral and ethical ramifications, as well as professional mandates that pull the service-learning practitioner into a jet stream of much broader and more complicated concerns. Beyond the impact that it has had on my classroom practices, service-learning has forever changed the way I view faculty roles, department and disciplinary conventions, and the institution of the university with respect to its service mission, not to mention my own professional identity. Since beginning to experiment with service-learning techniques in 1991, for example, I have developed a complete service-learning curriculum in my department that depends upon close partnerships with student services professionals, campus skills centers, and local community groups extending far, far beyond my department and college bases. At the same time, I have pursued a scholarship and research agenda integral to those curriculum development initiatives. It is an agenda that often materializes, in fact, in the concrete form of curriculum changes and adaptations as well as the more traditional research outcomes including monographs, book chapters, essays, articles, grant proposals, and conference papers. While those conventional forms of publication and research include work on service-based pedagogy, practice, and philosophy, service-learning has invited me to cross all sorts of boundaries as a scholar and pursue a line of research and writing into my disciplinary arenas of American Studies and Composition Studies and beyond: the tradition of the "Commons" in American public life, democratic theory, public philosophy, moral development, civic literacy, etc. I even have renewed energy and faith in academic organizations. While I still stay away from the Modern Language Association and the American Studies Association out of habit, I no longer cynically reject them outright, as I once did, as monoliths of professional pretense and self-congratulation. I have invested new hope in the work of, for example, the Invisible College, the National Campus Compact, and the National Issues Forum, and I am committed to and active in the service-learning community movement on my campus, my state, and regional collaborations in the upper Midwest. Moreover, I have become involved in many community organizations. I have answered the call of professional service by offering my modest talents as editor and writer to community groups, non-profits, and civic bodies ranging from the Michigan House of Representatives' Bipartisan Urban Caucus and Michigan Literacy Inc. to senior citizen centers and public housing advocacy organizations. My students are involved in many of these projects through their classroom-to-community assignments. As a happy result, the venue of my classroom frequently shifts between university buildings, hearing chambers, neighborhood centers, professional offices, and my van. A typical teaching day looks like a blur when compared to the tidy trail between a classroom with a lectern and chairs bolted to the floor and my office.

At the risk of overstatement, I have to say that the service-learning movement made me *whole*. It provided a lens, as Robert Frost put it in another poem, to "unite / My avocation and my vocation / As my two eyes make one in sight." It gave me a kind of template for professional integration just when I needed it to kick-start a career marked by enough conflict, separation, division, and isolation. Through service-learning, I was able to find a way to act on the integrative drives that accompanied my professional reprieve. Service-learning put Humpty Dumpty back together again by converging the separate pathways of scholarship, teaching, and service into the thoroughfare of an integrated professional and personal life.

More important, service-learning offers me a chance to answer the call of service to community and university that I heard after a long and frustrating period of isolation, moratorium, and crisis when I thought I'd never fit in. Like Thomas Merton, I came to grasp the full impact of the existential question "What will survive of me?", and service-learning gave shape, direction, and meaning to that generative drive.

Service-learning has also helped both to dampen and to temper my criticism of the theoretical excesses played out in the contemporary humanities with what I think is a decent measure of ethical accountability. As a faculty member involved in my community, I try to design justice-seeking assignments and community placements for my students that, whenever possible, bring democracy to bear on local groups for whom democracy has not worked well. I seek to immerse my students, and myself, in the pursuits—sometimes successful, often frustrating, seldom triumphal—of equal opportunity and social justice sought by sectors of American civic culture traditionally under-enfranchised: the mentally impaired elderly, for example, or economically dislocated single mothers and their children. At the same time, I am well aware of the ways political power is unevenly dispersed among social groups. In light of the new postcolonial scholarship, I also understand that history can be manipulated to enforce a phony pluralism that is coercive, not empowering. Far from being the problem, however, I believe that a vibrant, strong, viable civic culture is the best way to check the impulses to excess and inequity in our social and political arrangements.

Still, I try to gently encourage my humanities colleagues not to neglect the social primacy of the theoretical work currently dominating the academic scene. There is a real difference between radical theories of social transformation and cultural politics much in fashion in today's critical marketplace and the gritty spade work of democratic activism. A neglect of application and inattention to praxis—the bulwarks of ethical pedagogy and democratic change—make me uneasy about the arid material cranked out by an unselfcritical theory industry out of touch with human needs and interests. I have been especially hard on those who practice cultural studies and, girded by theories of cultural production and social construction, lay claim to the political utility and efficacy of their teaching without ever working up calluses or entering into the partial, diminished lives of America's discouraged underclass.

The struggle against intolerance, oppression, inequality, injustice, and exploitation will not be won at conference podiums, in academic journals, on Web sites, or, indeed, through the spiritually empty traces of theory. Instead, democratic reform, economic and social justice, and civic engagement have to do with ethical renewal and commitment. They require of faculty the same risks those faculty in the service-learning movement ask of our students: the risks of community involvement undertaken without expectation of personal aggrandizement or reward. The risks that accompany hope.

CONTRIBUTORS

Kurt Brandle is professor emeritus of architecture, University of Michigan, and member emeritus of the American Institute of Architects. His teaching, research, and practice comprise mainly building systems, energy conservation, and housing design. For many years Kurt has been involved with nonprofit organizations, especially the Washtenaw Affordable Housing Corporation in Ann Arbor, Michigan.

David D. Cooper received the Thomas Ehrlich Faculty Award for Service-Learning in 1999. He is senior faculty fellow for the Michigan Campus Compact.

Stephen L. Esquith is a professor of philosophy at Michigan State University and Michigan Campus Compact faculty fellow (1999–2000). His primary area of interest is political philosophy. Steve has written on such topics as political education, equality, war, and democratic citizenship.

Roseanne Hoefel, former associate provost and associate professor of english at Alma College, is the associate dean of the College of Letters and Science at the University of Wisconsin, Oshkosh. Her articles have appeared in *Studies in Short Fiction, Studies in American Indian Literature, The Emily Dickinson Journal, CEA Critic,* and *Transformations,* among others.

Margot Kennard is former director of the Academic Service Learning Program at Olivet College in Olivet, Michigan.

Myron A. Levine is W. W. Diehl Trustees' Professor of Political Science at Albion College. His writings include *Urban Politics: Power in Metropolitan America* (co-authored with Bernard H. Ross) and *Presidential Campaigns and Elections.* He has also written on the urban development policies of various western European nations. Presently, Myron is the head of the Albion City Planning Commission.

Virginia North is chairperson of the art and design department in the College of Architecture at Lawrence Technological University. She operates a consulting firm, North Design/Research. Virginia received a Ph.D. in architecture from the University of Michigan in 1991.

Nancy Wells is an environmental psychologist. She received her M.S. from Cornell University in design and environmental analysis, and a joint Ph.D. from the University of Michigan in psychology and architecture. Her research interests include the role of resident and volunteer participation in self-help housing programs, the impact of physical housing characteristics on the well-being of occupants, and the effects of the nearby natural environment on human functioning and welfare. Nancy is currently a post-doctoral fellow at the University of California, Irvine in the School of Social Ecology.